Khaled Nurul Hakim has a background in film and has claims to being the first homegrown BAME experimental writer in the UK. He took an extended absence from 2000 onwards, becoming a Sufi student and subsequently a Sufi musician.

The early published work is collected in *Letters from the Take-away* (Shearsman 2019). *The Book of Naseeb* was published by Penned in the Margins in 2020, and the early performative work is collected in *The Routines: 1983–2000* (Contraband 2021).

He is also the editor of *Weaving Light*, a retrospective of the work of artist-weaver Rezia Wahid MBE with contributions from poets and academics.

Khaled Nurul Hakim

*To the
Hitchhiking Dead*

Shearsman Books

First published in the United Kingdom in 2022 by
Shearsman Books Ltd
PO Box 4239
Swindon
SN3 9FN

Shearsman Books Ltd Registered Office
30-31 St. James Place, Mangotsfield, Bristol BS16 9JB
(this address not for correspondence)

www.shearsman.com

ISBN 978-1-84861-853-4

Copyright © Khaled Nurul Hakim, 2022
The right of Khaled Nurul Hakim to be identified as the author
of this work has been asserted by him in accordance with the
Copyrights, Designs and Patents Act of 1988.
All rights reserved.

Typesetting by the author.

CONTENTS

Introduction / 7

To the Hitchhiking Dead / 9

Doldrums 2020 / 13

Doldrums 1986 / 16

To the Hitchhiking Dead 1986 –
Holland – Germany – Vorarlberg – Belgium (?) / 18

Doldrums 1986? / 36

Doldrums 2020 / 38

To the Hitchhiking Dead – Ramadan 1987 – France / 41

Doldrums – Ramadan 1987 / 68

To the Hitchhiking Dead 1987? – (New York?) / 75

Doldrums 2020 – 2007 – 1987 / 80

Doldrums 1987 / 84

To the Hitchhiking Dead 1988 – Lands End / 92

Doldrums 1988 / 105

Doldrums 2019/2020 / 110

To the Hitchhiking Dead 20?? / 118

INTRODUCTION

To the Hitchhiking Dead is a book-length sequence culled from notebooks made between 1986–1988 when hitchhiking in Europe and England or otherwise doing nothing. An unknown poet – even to himself – who didn't know he was seeking and fleeing lost love, and assured he was the only Asian freak on the roads in nail varnish and pearls. Those notebook sketches were towards an epical rhapsody that never got written. By the time I came to be published in the '90s my poetry was framed in a post-Language discursivity: hard, vituperative, directed to actual audience-readers (epistles, performances). No-one would know that poet was made of such Romantic ravings.

When I belatedly, reluctantly returned to the insignificant poetry world after a protracted silence, I wanted to know what the vangardistes were doing these days. And I found a new online PDF zine produced in Seoul (*Erotoplasty*), and the very first poem in its first issue had a long poem called '*The A1*' by RTA Parker. It was like reading my abandoned poem, with the same cadences and Romantic visions. I later met him and told him there was no point to completing my poem. He demurred, and somewhere in 2019 I found I wanted to revisit the dozen notebooks to piece it together. Richard Parker wrote a version of my poem, and then I wrote my poem.

Returning to recover the project after 35 years sees a rapprochement between the two poet-selves. I am writing into the fragments of the past and the notebooks are writing into my occluded present. I've kept the scribal trace of each by retaining orthographic styles: I spelled conventionally before 1990 or so, and afterward determined on the course of unconventionalized spelling that has become signature to my work; so contemporary sections have deformed spelling but the original notebook writing is undeformed.

'*The Ballad of Geechie and LV*' with its themes of loss and seeking was written at the same time for Peter Riley's anthology *Last Kind Words*. I found *To the Hitchhiking Dead* spilling into that poem, and Geechie and LV writing into parts of this book.

KNH

TO THE HITCHHIKING DEAD

      You hitchers unbridled here
     all you Sabine women
    yoked to crumbling years
   clime up on yr sati faggots
  set lichte to a lyftime
shoplifting

take up yr wheelchairs
 you pantomime children!
  scour down the cirque
   carried on moraine
    run to the hitchhiking dead

      Muses, forgive
       Augustine, forgive me
        for indiscriminate haecceity
       for I cannot marry you

      All you fruits sweetened w/ sun
     you can save yr skin forever
    waiting for a fate
   flayed upon a plate
  but tell me you want to live
w/ yr feet up on the dashboard & I will kick out yr windscreen

Unclean spirits!

    take up yr tabor, babies; Da Mariae tympanum & cymbal
    take up yr tambourine Mariae w/out the legs,
      Ressurexit. Ressurexit.

& you, w/ the arm, Hector w/ a stick;

& one Sikh tabla, & a floor of tiny cymbalists
& the pots & pans of Gamelan

I want a brazen honk – crank it, ssshaake yr handicap,
sweat sweat. Im gonna boot yr wheelchair

we love him, we love her: for the neverending hips, & childbearing lips
& the cat squall, & his hurdle into agony

& most of all, the four electric bowed bass, whose undertow
& carbelt drone

If you only have five fingers, join w/ another,
there is no economy

Theres something wrong in everything
Accept the everything that hurts,
but dont accept the hurt
something wrong in the gap between song &

take yr earthly love & take it
where the unbelievers spill it all
its you we have to flee, yr words,
yr little devils; the horror is,
yre such little devils

To Hinny my hart:

A WON TOO FREE FORR

Ile tell y/ abowt 1985! It was spent w/owt a gold encrusted belt,
no spangly gold grit belt in that flat –

    that ane in Wycliffe Rd – that ane da landlord
    put my head thru th window
    that one yoo came to *herzling*

        a little gold flake belt & Yung Turk pantaloons –
        da one th black kids sed *You look lik a puff* –

    da one waere da Rastas torch Lozells as
    its thirs to torch – da wone
    were I look for lentils & th dealers
    smash up all th shops – all da racist
    Asian shops who hog th shops to themselvs –

Lets smash em up! **Hey I wanna smash em myself!**

No lentils! No **lentils in** my flat! I wuz th wone
the Indian landlord put my heod thru.

Lets burn sume **Asian shops** – dey're all racist!
    Not da post **offise**! Ive gotta cash me giro in there!

    No gold encrusted belt on this rode. No makeup remoover.
        No lihtbulbs in this post offiss.
            The poor Paki quizlings burnt alive.
                Still, ye cant compair dere oppression
            with a mob of blak & wite rioters –
        hooz side ar **they on**! –
    we can **hardly** throw a brick thru
the anlie saltfish patty shop

No belt on **Lozells Rd!**
    Wh**at ar** we angry abot!
        No frige in my frigde.
            Waeres Pogus Cæsar to tel th story. Did yu take
              a pictur of us burning dan th P.O. No racists on TV.
        Onlie a hafdead academic living in th skirting bords of
    Aston Universiti who had fortold ALL –
no harem pantaloons –
& if yoo dont giv us a living dole
to eke out my lipstick & sum drugs
    Im goona run down Lozells Rd & smash up
        any corner shop w/ a liyht bulb – any *chacha man* working
            18 hrs a day & fihting us off w/ a machete – da Rastaphobe
        racist!

            Whar ar yoo min heort!
           Im on the intersecsion of
              Villa Cross th betting shop &
                a gold encrusted disco belt
                & wimmens pantaloons.
              Only th Rock Aganst Lihtbulbs
            smashing up th Asian petit boorjwah!
            They look down on us Rastas.
        Espesially da Rastas w/ tortoisshell hareslides & Charleys
    Anjels hair.
        Espesially th wones w/ lentils.
            Take a pictur of *me* **Pogus!**

DOLDRUMS 2020

     waer doz it find yu lost *arhat* of erazure
    can y/ find him in yr 30 yr old hieroglyfh scraps
   lic a Rorshack moth engulfing a rag

 hes dere waiting for th richt tyme,
waiting for da rong lyftime, waiting for you
to start riting w/ a hand alredy taggd for a Gulag intern,
typriter balansed on a ledge

 any slip rode in th wind, any moterway in th sun, any moterway from
  heere to south, from midlans westward, heere to Scotland – I kno I
   went to Edinburugh that tym I crashd th Frinj – I no Im droppt
    on th ring rode utside Glasgow, & stood on a giant yland wiv
     da city in hot murk & full o fear & Gorbals tales, & deres
      even an Old Firm match n all.

   Ya ariht theer ma wee brown man. Ey Mary lass, com heere
    thun ya girly, gies a kiss ya littl puff.

    A motorway suth east suth west – I got a lift by
    three hells anjels or goths driving a pickup van, &
   þey tole me to get in the open bak. & th wind is beating
  me upsids, I think I tak th ships cap off & hair flayling.
  & I get an overhwelming funk dese Gothik redneck types ar
  driving me to my plase of tortchur. & da miles go by I see hem
læ3hing thru3 th bak window, & Im thinking I haf to stop dis truck,
I haf to kno…if I nock on da window & ask them to stop… then at lest
Ile kno. & th driver looks at me as if Im asking for a hot tub & TV in th
bak. & its too late to say, Oh never mind, Ile wait for sume poetri.

How did we get heere.
    Reeally.
        Evry tym I was on th Brent Cross
            sliprode I thocht of yoo my love.
                My brine eyd fate.
                Rolling a car into th canal.

        A self thats stitcht from fragments. A self dats blank
    to itself.

  Waere ar yu fate – I kno yore bak dere
 slowly killing me w/ sleep & wayting to pressgang me
into Yr Arms
O Lord
Whaer?
Hoo is this?
Evry second missing yr wyf,
evri second flaking off her & rolling
into dunes of skin under th bed, everi second
 missing everi second, every wyf wedged into a carpet of haire
  in th hoover then scraped into a plastick bag by th haples huzbond –
    everi huzbond a broken vacuum clener da wyf cant throw away
    Yallah my *beti*!
   Beti mor than *beti*,
     spurnd & spurning *heti*!
  I wish yud had my babiz,
 da way I had yr babiz.
God, Yu had my babiz?
You had all ower babiz?
Yu had all owr comings &
ower strayings & ower brekfasts
& owr lie-ins & owr worn-owt shoos & car battriz

O Raðhu Allahu anhu wa raðu an
O Raðhi morr than *janam*
roll me up into a Godshapt ball of *gulabjam*
hold me but not too tiht
hold me but not too liht,
hold me Allah lyk yu mene it
hold me lyk yore *Ahad*
GODDAMMIT GOD I LOVYU!

DOLDRUMS 1986

                      do y/ want to now wat I did
                  after rioting – do y/ want to
              now wat I did after th landlord –
          da won who put my hed thru –

    I ran away from yoo to Bangladesh
      w/ mom – to ficht off marrige w/ my familie
    I heard I gav my cuzins my charity shop shirts –
  I ran away from my moðer w/ you
  I ran away w/ Samantha from you
    she ran away w/ a smackhed from yu
      I ran from marrij until it ran from me –
      then I ran to marrij till I was cawht
      & evry day deres no escape

      ye keep looking in th mirrer but yore stil
    thare –
  doomd to rome an alien landscap whaer
  evrything is comforting & familier –
  a dog a hog a slowboild frog
  dat keeps turning rownd & rownd
its tale hoping to find its plase –

  Run run run, beever tootht Pasha
 run to yr lost sandles in heafon, to th imprint of a beeche
in Yugoslavia a honied licht in Clawde glas, to th beutifull slavs
w/ ugly slav hands

I beleev I was impregnated by alienz w/ an imaje of home:
an imacculat lizard princess hoo may hav had sex w/ me. I

was probably 11 at th tym, & it waz just after going to see
Cinderella, & I remember th radiantly fuzzy avatar hovering
over me at niht, & drawing owt my life forse. After that no
wunder I failed my exams.

Run run run rolling beetel
a litel wooden boy w/ rickets
a litle wooden boy w/ a litle wooden heort
a littel woody pecker
enogh to mak a kitszlich kindling
enogh to leve a splinter in yr crak

drag a carcass of poetrie acros deenatured landscap
flay it of proceedur reeding radical cant
no oulipian alibi larded w/ continentel fuckery
on a leesh of lov leding me to say it say it say
aaaAARRGHH SAAy
heere w/ my nervs
out ut ut in th pissy sae
sooo faaar

   take a foot,
      a slender
         longitudinal
            arch w/ monky toez –
               take won step take another

        Im gonna run after th Frend til he lyes down
          exawsted & I wawk up & speere him – speer YOU sweethart
w/ yr eyez th color of clowds rolling bak, saying *Do it qwickly*!

Im gonna run after God till I lay down hopless, saying
pleeze dont hurt me!

TO THE HITCHHIKING DEAD 1986 – HOLLAND – GERMANY – VORARLBERG – BELGIUM (?)

how did I get here –

a ferry deck as brilliant as Botticelli wavelets.
Flying by on a mission, a crisp packet.
The bright mists of midday.
The wind picked up & shooed
him off deck.

Ive been to Harwich Ive bin to Dover Ive travelld this blank
zone all over,
over over,
dedd in clover,
throw yrself overbord an swim
to Hoek van Holland

I was laughing on a sliproad under fantastic poisonous pillars
of the M1, for a lift that never stops. & hayfever.
w/ nothing nothing
nothing nothing
w/ th siren calling east that I may somehow founder south
a dream that fades before it admits it wants cloudy contrary desires
look into the wrinkled English Channel & see
the limitless dyed jean water of Bodensee

I want to see Yu Allah,
charging bosons into Wirld,
I want to see You w/out a book,

                    a ferry reeled in on a fishes littel hook,
                    a thrælll of luf þat th wirld mistook,
                    my triple row of pearls & kommandant look
                the only requisite you look gullible

        Here I am, sailing to old nuts.
        Does anyone have the empty instinct.
The ditherer, not I, not now: like searching for yr menopause
what broken fibs go under the floorboards

How did I go to Rotterdam to Amsterdam how did I get to Ostend.

                    Dis boy is a blank, a girl in want
                        of a woman, a blank to all
                            exsept da genteel woman
                                whod never seen a grave boy in perles

                        this want forgot to mark th passige
                    confused w/ th same
                retreeting tracks
        of an animal hoo chewd
his paw owt of th trap.

            A ride from Rotterdam
                    to Amsterdam in dusk –
                        to land in night – another
                            park bench sleeping on my
                                bag where the kids creep up
                                    & I scare them off –

                or is it a ride thru dawn bruised purple

>   another ride to Amsterdam
>   to walk silent bike lanes to a bank of sedge,
>   an erection the size of the landscape – the last time
>   it cried for you in all virility

O Khaled Crimplene, yr trousers are still in Handsworth

& as soon as I landed in the empty square I snapped into action – I buy some acid off a lowlife who sees me coming. He wants to sell me Es but I'm not having that – so I scurry away w/ my piece of card hed ripped off, & I look at it, & I know I've spent half my money on half of a Jack of Diamonds; but I'm thinking maybe the diamonds are the acid. I still ate the card.

The bicycle thieves boltcutting chains in libertarian heaven.

In heatwave Europe I hook up w/ two older gays, & gave them half my hayfever tablets – they kept passing all the models windows w/ the rivers of tourists & saying, But its so charming! (I see y/ hords shuffel down Brick Lane saying, Its so charming!) – tha distingwishd biznessman assess th coqett in her bra & I say Thats me!

O Khandan, all I want is to find y/ in th canal, or in the errant sentrybox canal houses dat cock a snook at th richt angels of modernizm – won bulldozer, won revolucion in shitgrade concreet!

In Amsterdam I threw a pizza slice backhand into a letterbox.

Unlearn fearful magic.

A man w/ his head smashed open down the steps of a barge – luckily he doesn't know he's got a head. One false move & this poem is dead. & time to move.

With nothing nothing
nothing

    a ride to Aachen,
        a ryde thru Aachen
           & th dreme of borderles being –
              a ryde thru3 da histori of dreming,
                  da boundary of being & th sticks o tribe,
                      a ryde thru3h slavery & dryving, a dreme
                          of histori dizolved in a broken subject
                              rapt in a sack w/ three ferrits
                      a ride thru da treatyless garden fense
            in a bownded bodie historicizd
        & dehistorisized into nocht
driving to clowdy eidolons wreckt w/ yr fool face

Essen,
      Köln,
           Koblenz –
                pullulating Freaks –
to the backward hollows of Hessen

Hessen.
Pray y/ never go
whare yu walkt th burning sholders of de Reich, & at any tyme thoz
autobaan Polizie culda sd *Get in,* insted of saying *Yu cant hitch heere* –
protected by stupidity or perles. Those fucking burgher dicks,
passing,
passing,
thousands of them,
thousands of them,
while I dessicate in a heatwave w/out water or food
any torrid zone, any trucker w/ a broke tachometer

Im standing heer, w/ wyde cornfield & aotobahn intersexions, so
uncomprehending, þat cackkneed hominids walkd ut of a cresscent,
walking 4 kilometers an hr, & seen da forest perennials & th hills & slag,
& th slav forse slappt down a leveling faster an I can walk, mils of it,
mils & mils.

A burocrasy of rolling stock, gipsys, contracts, Juden
þe advansegard caked & despoiling lome on th splintering forest front,
hwil hinten is da beutifull blak tarmacadam dreme, as my crawling
ilegally along da freaks way

dreming Aston Cross,
you grate concreet canal, w/ th circits of th flying M6: this is how I
luve: under me at any tyme, going to Afrika.

Hwere slæpst þu suna. Away frum eigen & ratten. And Allah is Rahman.

I spent 2 days shuffling between
     Heidelberg,
       Wiesbaden,
  some place,
           Darmstadt.
        Then finding my way back,
    landed in the night this tenth dimension.
  I spent 50 hours, for like 6 lifts.
There were. No freaks.

A morning I cudnt go on & clymbd over rails down th concret starway
of th floodbank, & lay back in a swoon…

So we'll be water held as pectin in a desert anemone
to be used in one burst after 20 yrs
all the muscle mass of salmon

as real as Norman Wisdom singing lieder

as a sleepwalker must go on dreaming

  lest he fall
    landing on the other side
      of the customs, thinking to all
        the Bavarian burghers:
           Ive come to plough yr kine…

a motorway station where I ask the boy how much for the big bottle of water, coz Ive kept an English tenner, and he says something exorbitant, and Ive turned away, & maybe it was the girlfriend w/ him – because he calls me back and straight out gives me the bottle.

It's 35 years & I realize I was 2 hours away from hospital on a saline drip.

          Who was the boy.
          Who was the girl.
         Do you remember
        an emaciated Indian
       in a U-boat jacket &
      three rows of pearls over
     the soft mat of my chest.

And a lift wif a cheery biznesman in his BMW just ut of th garige w/ 2 other boy scowts in da bak who lookt lyk theyd just bin sucking him off, & an Ozzie bloke. & th driver sd, Ok, lets just see – & he floord it on th Chansellors awtoban & I saw th dial goo up to 170-180 & he held the engin wailing till he had mercie & eazd off.

I sez to the Ozzie kid, Its funny, I was convinsd I was going to end up
mangeld by a car, & I cd never not be belted. & now heere I am in the
object of my fears w/ my feet up on th dashbord doing hundreds of
mils in lorriz w/ no belt. & he sd *Yu can think yrself into that wish.*

& th merry buzinesman is asking me waer Im going & whare Im
staying, & I think I was crypticly Dhammapadaish, lyk I think he was
maybe
inviting me to meet his famili, but my Grasshopper puritie
wont alow me to deeviat from th rood – Allah yoluna
  just to go strai3t & say no matter how stupid
     & he sez Ah, I think I understand –
        yre a masokhist!

            From Ulm – to hwere?
              I had to wait w/ calcined lips
                  for another rodeside hitch –
                      a woman who stops & flufs
                          her curls in th drivers mirrer
                              as I run up w/ my bag – & I
                              wil never able to drink my
                            dryness back –
                          no no, it was th biznesman –
                      this last nicht bifor I crawl into
                Freedrichshafen – & so I was invited
        to dinner wif da mans wyf & sister –
th last dawn burn bifor I wawk
into yr funny trees –

& th sister in law is telling me how she bicame vegetarian – how she
fond a cat that was hafdedd & she got a big stane & – bah! – finisht it,
Its better that way.

Im so tired so tired – a bony cat w/ blanchd muth – I must hav slept at th mans haus w/ his familie – so tired

How did I cume to you in th morning – Im cuming to yu greenfingerd betrayer!
  Im coming to y/,
    absent pantheist,
      I see yr insooscience
         & I raize yoo ignorans,
I dont even no yuve been closer to me than my jugular vain

Hu am I kidding, yr þihs ar spred fra Konstanz to my bed, yr criez wil reche me in another centurie, & I can onli mak sense of it wacching Fury beet up Wilder over & over agen

& th customs guards werent going to let me in – I thought it was a wasted ships captain look, but they thought it was a drug dealers look. I kept on saying Im staying in Hochheinem. They kept saying they never heard of it. I think I got it mixed up w/ a motor race track.

Here I am walking in gingerbread Bregenzerfeld. With the bike slopes & heat.

Ðen he smashed a cat.

Because providence told me. A test brought to me. When he threw the stone & shut his eyes, he thought hed never forget the amazed horror as the cat stretched agape to heaven & groaned. That he shd have done such a thing.

I think it was drowsy w/ dying, in my ditch to cloudy, a rasping flyblown thing already claimed by undergrowth. Flies flew in its eyes. A slug trying to get into its mouth: was it refreshed.

I tried to pull its tail in a tissue, out of the drain; & it hissed faintly. & I stood w/ a big stone.

Then the woman came out to see the gypsy weirdo at the bottom of her mountain garden. & when she understood she sd: Iss spesser. Iss spesser.

I toed its head into position & threw down the stone, & it scrabbled & went *Wooaaw*, & it lolled & panted. & I took up the stone & tried to get its reddened head to lie there, & I threw it again. & the cat w/ its flies was not dead or quiet. & I threw my hands to God.

When I banged its head this time, its eyeball shot out & it stretched like steel & this was the end.

This is for a cat.
Now Im cuming down th mountin.
 Dear Lord,
  Dear Lord,
   Dear Lord, Dear Lord

    That I. That people. Help me Lord.
    Never.
    From such.

   Father in Heaven who died.
   Father in heaven. Who died.
  Father who creates all things. & died.

Even enfeebled moggy. Forgive me. I did right, & its still wrong.
Only you know what I do, right or wrong.

The popping eye looked at me.
I thought of Greeks.
Who grow awry, as parents.

I wæs thar in Evas haus w/ her new mann – a spare man w/ an
interest in Wilhelm Reich, th usual communistick retreet for da
sudentenland jugend wheraz I want to liv in Aryan faeryland –
w/ her cast iron bike
    w/ da basket,
        w/ th gang sunning
           on Bodensæ concreet
        w/ a girl from Insbruk
    loytering by lik a coy shoplifter
  O Khandan whare were yoo
O *Beti*, who was I seeing
when I spok w/ yu –
whos jeens patcht
  w/ needelpoint,
      whos swimsute drying
        under her cloze that day
          theze desiccatt legs
              that cauze amazment
                at St Gallens
            w/ you

            the dark runnel
        from the sunset tipping forward
      & lifting his breaststroke; pulled
    to the red sun on the diesel blue, &
      the breaststroke goes as easily
          as swimming to suicide.
            They lap his mouth,
                  swimming to Switzerland

                    to Lichtenstein; then he loses
                            the spell, & the water chokes,
                                            & he's too far.

                                            Look back.
                            The black & white figure
                on concourse, he strokes towards
            some muzzy thing, w/ the runnels
      chopping over him, & his failing rhythm.
Till God come & bound like a scull.

a wind starts up, & he dries his bare bum, mesmerized on fretted
shield, wide waters, wide waters, & stippled blanket. His eyes as wide
as the lake.

She watches him, but he is mesmerized fretted shield
She offers him breakfast tomorrow.
She shakes her head –
he shook his head.

That impuls to push th bondes of diction
to push th bondes of a frend into vasselej

evry evening Id com bak from breststroking Bodensee & get ut of my
hed on fennel tea –

You know one of these days Im going to swim out & get cramp, & Ile
be too embarrassed to glug for help

I tell you Pregnant One, all you got to do is go down the boardwalk,
all the ambition in the world goes down the boardwalk

To get you on my knees

I was puushing y/ too hard I was pushing yoo –
maybe wait until th ssummer diies
maybe waait until th ssummmer –
but waiting for another lyf
lasts a lyf tiiime

I cam to Yor gingerbred clocks of Lindau; da piney montain lacs yr
parents luved to go; þat y/ took me after an lyftyme; dat lac I cant
remember after an lyftime

I cam to y/, th same hills seen from yr haus, or at lest Evas haus, &
I expected God to send y/ a messige, to hop on th train & get sume
kidneyz from da posh butcher: Im waiting dere. Im sunbaðende on da
concreet esplanad, 2 sticks of rubarb for legs & an Adams appel w/ perls.
Im wayting for y/ to stop me straying w/ sume *beti*, expecting God to
rite th wirld aronde us, & fold ower pages so we meet.

20 yrs 20 yrs, always th dezert teks 20 yrs

It is a strainge dezert dat looks lyk this – w/ shops & banks & cildren
w/ names: ye cd freeze this town for 20 yrs – a Layli cutting vegetabels
& Majnun hiding in lofts – it took deth to waken, it alwayz taks deth to
waken, it taks a 19 yrs old dying of her tumer to bring me joy, a Manna
returnd to Heofen, it teks a fader who has to die of cancer so I can cume
to yoo –
& yu sd
whare th Hell were You all my lif –
too full of Mercy, too full of Merci to kill anywon els

hwy dozent God send a rippel of perturbacioun from my sashay on th
Bodensee, from my bike in th Bregenzerfeld

Hey Layli!
Yr stupid pridefull lapdog has cume for yr begfull kisses

Why didnt the Univers kno hwat to doo –
it left us 20 yeres naither faithfull nor untruu
then brings us to mak luve on yr fatherz deethbed
& left Majnun in th parking lot
   as she fled for th scool run,
     & hee for th last tyme ran for her 4 hweol drive

the onli time he ran for her

I left yoo, furry green Vorarlberg, clowdy in heet & fertilizer, in my blisters & sæ capten look, w/ 50 marks from Evas Mum who thot it was an Aids victim look

      walc onto another
     broiling petrol forrcort,
    w/ an opentop red Ferrari
    & tannd blond gigolo in
    da pasenger seet, & dis long
     darkhærd model cumes ut of
      th forcort shop – & I no its not his
       but I stil ask him Can I get a lift,
        & he nods to th model in th short
         red evening dress, & shes very nise,
          sheell let me get into th tiny rear
           for half a lift. I bet she was a
            pornstar – sumwone famus –
            possibly th most famos person
            I hitch wif till I meet Fred West.

    Im thinking Hwat if she didnt haf beefcake,
   hwat if she needed a dehydrated pool atenndant –
  wat if dey both want Asian poontang – hwat if she wanted
to fuk me in a cellar hwil he cuts my fingers off.

I dont gno how many byrds got wasted in th grille of a car or lorry
scatterd on th raads, but a linnet got suckt into th radiator of an lorri &
flung ut at My feet to die exawsted w/ Me

& wait w/ calcened lips
 for another servis stacion hitch –
  a woman who stops & fluffs her curls
   in th drivers mirrer as I run up w/ my bag –
    & I wil never be able to drink my dryness bak –
  an English hippie hoo spoke morosly
 of hicching in America full of fukking
 qweers
any torrid zone,
any trucker w/ the same idea

You on the rood
You all I want
Its a long way back to Germany
Its a long way back to Germany –

For almost my last pickup
 of wankers Belgium,
  Im lucky w. two real Freaks.
   Was it mongrel Flemish.
   The driver, the cool one,
    as I admire thr faded tattoos

                    to keep them sweet, he signs
                    to me theyre on hashish &
                    mainlining smack.
                The baby brother, retarded, is
                  whooping at the evening drivers.
              & were doing 120 as they knock bk
          Pils & bottle the motorway: rocking
    the radio to Shakin Stevens. Im thinking
this is it. It wd be a pleasure to be robbed
by these –
Im too knackered.
My fear is theyll invite me
to stop the night.

Hwær slepst thu suna. Aweg fra eigen
& ratten. And Allah is Raheem.

From Blankenberg walking the giant dunes to Ostend,
                    or was it Dunkirk in birdsong,
                        the sand stacked high as breakers

                        þis beche w. no bizines except
                    a plezant costal walk to somwhær
                & a subject mooving in a moving landscap
a landscap þat wil filter other bodiz, hærless dark bodiez
drawn w. *rooza* trekking up fr Levant or Maghrib,
in better jeans dan me, cuming in a *mi'raj*
to a sexy shelf of Slavic sand

  coming fr another wirld
      to da 'fatal avenu',
          to mass at þe
              fortifyd ports,

        theyr hiking þis dune raad,
          þe trains & botes & da lorriz, to get to me

a blak silhowette in a Caspar Freedrich shorr,
wayting for th train or bote or plane þat took me away from you,

& if a prayr can tunnel th sæ
      to bring England to him,
         þat took yu away from me

    bifore my final silens,
      working in a 2nd hand electrical shop
as Sufi penanse, & Id stand in ða bak hwar the Afghani is fixing a
clappt out washing mashin, & telling me his ride to London in th
petrol tank of a lorry,

               & tels me his first storie
                 getting to uncnawen
                   hellzone in Russian winter,
                 waer th smugglers dropt him
               & th 2 Bangladeshi breððers
             into the erly howers of a frozen
        wast,
      to wait for
    da next rendezvus w. a smuggler pickup;
& told to keep running
    aronde da feelds, keep
        mooving or yle die,
        keep moving till
          da truck or van
            turns up —

    & Ahmed
   keeps jogging, for how
  lang – for a vehical dat may or may
  not cume, in th bak of nowhar – but ða
  Bangladeshis slow down in unfathomabl
 cold,
cant keep going, so drawn to acing pese,
so drawn to sleep in Allahs lap, hwere
ane bredder can lay bac in da bushes
 burning w. sleep –
  Oh bha, oh bha, ghoomayo na, khobodda,
   ghoomayo na! – Na bhaiya, ami farram
    na, ami toora aaram kori…tumi
     soloh, soloh…

      is þat me deed w.
     my Reynawds fingers
    & bad sirculacion, or
   am I still shuffling
   shufling ronde
  w. Ahmed –
keep moving
 keep moving –
  hwar ane broðer
   se lieʒ him in blissfull
    hypothermia in da roots,
     & another bruðer trys
      to jog unfathomabel
       snaw,
     & Ahmed
     keeps tredding
    ane morr step of lyf,

      lic a steorfende creture,
     lic a lame steorfende deor,
  ontill da polis cam & find hem –
Ahmed hoo has run a frozen lyf tyme ronde his circit, & ða breððers lost in snaw,

lost ontill th spring thaw, w/ut a name or word, lost to a familie hoo can never be trased nor heare another word

      Come home battered.
       Yr little bark, lost
        Every joy &
        tender one
       in the bacchanal

     A farewell to correspondence.
    Some kinship practice of daughters
    in exogamous exchange, some marriage
   arrangement between maternal brothers
   all the unsung father-satyrs & seraglios
  of neurosis all the runaways for affection
 who shall go thru making misery
is it for these, my promiscuously
 beautiful kind
  for these
   untutored dreck –

  it is for these

DOLDRUMS 1986?

There was, corn moon coming out the backward tree again:

                  In the bathroom
              the miraculous 2 panes
          of dimpled glass, a commanding
        lumen
     of Jibreel,
a double trumpetmouthed cylinder
   splaying out,
     that carried the curve
       of its flattened rim,
         round in the great globe,
           the double axe brightness
             in grey halo –

                over a crumple
             of lights deforming houses
         lamp posts; & in it corn of lesser
        trumpetmouths; & at the left pane a
       ghostly smear of cylinder,
                    that curved
             into the head as streetlamp
         big elliptical aureole, flaring
             into an orange

what conjuring of nature are y/ seeing
You, on the rode, you all I want
It's a long way back to Germany
It's a long way back to Germany

God help us, in the clutch of the shadow tree — Ive been here before
She takes it out on the kid, I take it out on the wall. & we get along
Give it a rest! Give it a rest willya! & even the kid untouched

Burn the memories.
w/ all the faces covered in golden fuzz

    next doors momma thrashing the cherubini
      Yre old enough to understand! Right! Right! —

   keep it up ya frigging whacko
   bringing up fuckups
  How can I be
 darling as
 Englebert
 Humperdinky
  thrashing next doors tots
   Ahh there there there
     send yr injured feeling thru
      the passage, doors
     open the doors,
    enter the room.
  Look at it
the red glow of cigarette, the complicity
this girl, this boy

ye Rhiney spooks, protect yr changelings
even at the checkpoints
suffer the little porkchops
all those ghostly runaways
fingered by their family
whove never run away in weeks

DOLDRUMS 2020

Im trying to find my plase, to shelv away. But th *distans* is so far:
theze yrs of catabasis – gon bk to rescew th legless fallen notbooks
th fleeting heroz hwa flicker wones on th carousel –

a reeking 2 up terrase burnt owt by th landlord identical to th ane I
haus sit, hwer I crashd w. Nichtmare, & Mad Graham w. a dildo bends
over & open up his anus, & Nichtmaer la3fs & seyz Stick it in him.
Whaer th landlord tryd to smoke them ut

Ni3tmaere, looking lyk a greenhæred scullery maide for the Addams
Family – y/ cd be my dole offiser
I shar her sleeping bag, & Graham lowing
Yoo shd be in here w. me –

      yu ar still utside th flæe market
    ane last tym deep in Iron John
     hwere I betray y/ & walk on by
       for the last tym,
        y/ ar still in a motorway verg in th nicht
          & lying ther *reely crying,*
         Becuz somtims Ray,
       its gd just to reelly cry,
     & ane day my tyme worm & yr tym worm
   wil meet on th same rode
  to enchanted Yugoslavia
but whoz gonna pick up a 7 ft Harleqwin?

why do y. attend to yr own cry
cantiga de amigo

precisely in those older restricted forms
Ai cervas do monte; vin vo-lo dizer:
out of all license that cannot be done:
a shape of stardust & a summer beetle
running around the floorboards; Gerrow of it!
why dont you cry enough:
there are some things y. cant say right: turned into ptry too soon
to find Khandan in a courtesan & find a courtesan in love,
why do you attend to yr crying
its got nothing to do w. anyone

You hitchers to unbridled years
yu ded ungulats
looking for a good scool for th girl
yu dedd poltroons –
take up yr wheelchair,
run to th hitchhiking ded in perles
steal a plowshare & drive it off th cliff into th Gt War
disinter the impertinant pulss

a notbook w/ a crying clowd
a prezent that th past alowed
a cild to yr cildren
a father hoo wil diee well

a mann is a wether-vane
twisting in a wyf
a pritti ball & chain
w/ a pritty litel knife
a *beti* dobbly jelus
for her unbownd thrall

Muses, forgive
Augustine, forgive me
an indiscriminate hussy
that cannot marry you

she is what I am not
clouded in Calais,
clouded in loading bay,
looking for dawn burns
dismorfia of plase þat seeks to fit eche vista onto a lingering dreme of
slavick dunes come rorring fr da channel lik Afrikan bees

TO THE HITCHHIKING DEAD
– RAMADAN 1987 – FRANCE

When I asked mom for the money to go on the Norfolk Broads trip, she didn't say anything. She got the money. I heard there were boys in tears at the thought of bunking up w/ me.

They know, who loves the sun, loves the flies.

        So in the great ploughing stern,
           theres a pull to the methereating
                  sea,

     & add yr drops to the sea, because
    ye want to join all the
drops
  the sewer coloured
    rising milk of mind
      a jump in to join all the drops

        Almost at the same time
         a Welsh farmer kills a child
          & escapes to Dover where he
         hitchhikes down to Lyon:

        who was he fleeing to –

      A memory of landing
    in Dunkirk or was it Calais
  a memory hoping to find yr love
in the wrong country

    a hitchhiking notbook
     dat rides th hippocampus
       acros da waves to meet yu al
           in Paris or dementsia,
             & fals apart

                    a ferry dat waits for yu on the M1
                    & gooz a hundred wayz
                    to slip yr fate
                    yore too
                    late
                son,
                yre too late

        Calais was already closed.
      Breaking fast w/
    a cheeseroll
   in a doorway.
 Protected by Ramzaan
& a tuperware tub of bodibilding proteen.
This poem is too long.

     & the dusk is over the rapefields.
      I was hiking down the road for 2 hours
         w/out sight of houses & I get to this roadside cafe bar,
        & Im plucking the courage to ask for mineral water,
      & they come piling out like a clan to sort the Gyppo
    trying to nick their Honda – Haute! Haute!
  And these Flems were going to do me
but maybe I sounded like
an English fairy.
  & I get shoved off.

                    An hour up the road
                            in this farming plain like
                        twilight North by North-west,
                            & these headlights come up
                        & instead of going by & stopping
                            & me running to the brakelights,
                            it stops w. me in the headlights,
                            & I knew I was in trouble.

            & I walk a bit closer to ask like
        is he going further. & the voice is saying
Ja ja, ja ja.

I know hes from the cafe, come to
                entice me proper,
        come to do the English gyppo fairy,
        come for Asian poontang – & I start walking on ready
to run into the black fields if they charge me out of the headlights.

                                    But this
                                isn't what it's about.
                            It's about this field of hectic
                        rapeseed like a hallucinogen;
            & this mother of an arc-lit powerplant
        the size of a town
            that took an hour
                to walk in windy drizzle.

                    Midway to Bologne from a 5 km lift,
                                Allah lets it piss.
                            Standing in a shopdoor.
                        The street lights go out at half 11.

Eating *sehri* w/ a cheeseroll & protein shake, waving the Pigs on by. This is the tricky part of finding a place sheltered & unsoiled.

Sleeping unseen in a supermarket bay w. the lorry lights unloading thru the night, on a wooden pallet w. the rats ripping at my trousers & shoes, nipping at the corners of a raincoat thrown over the shy bride's head

35 years later to realize the hauliers cd have unloaded a halfton crate on my head

telling th rats to Fuck off from under my winding sheet – waiting for clowdy dawn burns that never cume

Limping for Paris it pissed down. For who loves the sun loves the rain. I wd have been dead w/out Pete's raincoat – for every decision is the right one.

& I get dropped off some control point in the pour, where no sun looks, & if I stand in one lane the lorries arrive in the other: but for this rain, Im going to stick it w. my mac. But the checkpoint Super moves me from the shelter: so it may pour untroubled.

I wont move. *Vull morir en pelag d amor*

Till I go to the shelter, and a van pulls up:
   Hey man are you English.
      Well they're Scottish.
         To Reims to Reims!
           Where's Reims.
              It's about 5 km
                 past Paris.

> My trousers were so wet
> my groin was burnt black
> w. the friction.
>
> Did I ride to Reims just to dry out.
> But then I wdnt have had
> the lift back to Soissons
> w. the bloke who told me
> the first story:

I pick up a boy – like you – coming fr Soissons he sd he was 16 &
hes going to meet his brother. & its late so I invite him to stop w. my
family

& in the morning I gave him 50F & sd if he ever was in trouble…And
after a week maybe, he was back, & he sd he was only 14 & he didnt
got a brother. His parents they threw him out
you can be strong w. foreign parts
you can be weak & be strong to come back
but walk out of the auditorium
walk for a kiss

& he run away fr the state institution to ask his parents to take him
back but they throw him out & he was going back to the institution
when I pick him up. But a boy he told him there was a chance he wd
go to jail. So he asks me if there is anyway to help him. So I let him
stay & I went to the authorities. The judge sd he can be in my custody
for a week. & so, he stayed.

When I first knew him, he was very rough. He never did anything, my
wife and children they sd: only w. me is he gentle. Once there were
guests, & you shd shake hands & rise for the ladies, & he ignores them:

& at the table he rudely demands. When they left, I took him & sd that he must say Please. & the boy he sd No, Ile never do that.

& next day he sd Alright, but only to you. & so little by little... 3 times he was caught shoplifting, & I went to the police station; & pleaded w. them not to withdraw custody – it was better he was out of dentention; & it was only because I knew someone in the administration

& so slowly the boy become family. & he stayed till – when did he say – 22, 23. He married. Hes living in Lyon. Hes 28 now. Or no. So now when his children say or do wrong things, hes the first one to come down.

Though Im going to Soissons.

> Man the driftwoods for me, children
> Its me, a pantomime horse
> asking refractory gendarmes
> if they know a cloudyshaped hole
> an invisible cloud of patisserie
> flaunting itself
> from Nord Gard
> the breathtaking
> smells of Montparnasse
> w. nothing but my ferry return

when I landed in Pigalle to stay w. Isa & her kid – an Isa Im assured by M I know – she must have suspected in the three days I stayed there that we had never met

& anyway she told me about her friend, who on the Paris streets at 5 o clock in daylight,

& this fou attacked her & started raping her, & everyone can see, & nobudy did nuffin, they all cd see & just walked by. & the man got up & just walked away; & she then walked to the hospital herself because it was not far & nobudy helped. It was in all the papers. How this cd happen w. everybudy around. & like a woman sociologist she sd that people had become so conditioned to watching everything on TV, that they cdnt stop thr passive

whereas I , who instantly feel the freezing numbness of real life, sat watching the Cannes festival w. flu, till ejected back into the rain –

but Ive cume to th rong Paris for my clowd –

    & now dere is only th march
        of þe Cildrens Crusade
            to da Holy Land,
              a cildrens armie
                hitchhiking to
              th Holy Land
          to be sold into slavery
þe *peurti* who left dere plows,
left dere frendes, the elect of poverti
who find da phatick shepherd boy

        to leve da boss
      the appoyntments
    da paranoid streets
th rape alarm
    & fling yorself
      into Gods care
          seying I doo beleev,
           coz I bileeve in Yoo,
         Oo–oh oh,
         oo oh oh oo-oh,
          I bileave in You

     & find there are
     2 kinds of people –
    those
   who give y/ a lift,
   & those who dont
  & find there is life after shampoo

Where am I – is it Blankenberg in the night or some outskirt of Bologne or Sutton Coldfield, where the shadow in a black mac is shuffling along & a shiny saloon car pulls up ahead, & the door opens as I go by on the grass verge & keep going –

perhaps noone knows were all going to Jerusalem

but if y/ hadnt met that boy in the Paris station you wdnt have got a lift to Port d Italie, & if y. hadnt got kicked out by that queer feeling y/ up you wdnt have been nowhere at midnight & got that grace of doing distance

 the characters never go for a piss,
   but Ile help yr wheelchair into the howdah
    & sing yoo ditties hwil
     they pottytrain
      th palseed

    this businessman gives me a lift,
   Im wondering how far,
   & hes making chitchat
  & then he says Is that nail varnish,
 & starts w. the stroky stroky.
I still dont know how he saw
my Baby Pink varnish in the night.
 Fucking nonce.
  But when I demur I get dumped.

        & when graced by the long ride
           what did you see in night as the
               road keeps the curve of disembodied
                   white lines along the edge of a world,
                       we read just enough of the world
                           to follow for hours

             Again. & again. & again.
               The same poem
       Again. & again. & again.

do you know this psycho in the car —
do us a favour — kill him
stars in yr windscreen
   as rainpearl riding a windscreen
      on the yellowsaucered ride
          w/ every headlight ribboned into night
                     river of brakelights
                     river of flight

              any torrid zone
              any truckers w.
            the same idea
           in a Hannibal cabin
        mowing down the little eskimos

     Join the Moonies, theyll give you a good time
     falling in ditches w. frozen cantos

     Lyon — Im coming to yr trial
        in the bow of a lorry w. Beethoven
           this happiness of 40 tonnes
            along

>   the edge
>   of the world
>   join the true fatalism
>   of Baghdad lorries
>   smoking on a melting road
>   tearing the common bread
>   of our thin uncoddled bodies

She is what I am not –
her body
   an electric charge of latex
      th pull of ower genes together,
         my beutie & yr beeutie as we stood in a slav market
        & hoped to be sold together
       fighting to stop the car –
       I must be dreaming –
       I am dreaming!

       All my decisions are right.
      Yes we are going to Cote d Azur.
     Yes we will avail of my shaven legs.

as in a layby in his considerate French, across our sleep, he explained the course of perishables at night which can only be taken by truck at a constant 5%: Cest probleme

for say, at the monumental doublemouth of Lyons, a jam shd poison the fruit. These are the bands which run Nord Sud across our sleep

    & in the late dawn
   we are getting into Provence,
  tho I cant keep my eyes open

Lyon, hazy on the hill, beseiged
  on the Marseilles route,
    Lyon rivered, w. the refinary
      & industrial dumps:
          Ile whitewash you!

        My driver winds up
          a forest brow:
            & must find
              his orders depot
                  where theyll help
                      unload
                  where I must piss —
              a wide warehouse bay,
            & Audi plant.

          Cest probleme:
        by one minute —
      hes just had a call
    from his boss —
by one minute
I missed getting to Avignon
  but hes just had a call from his boss
        to pick up a load at Dijon. Wch is Nord.
            The poem is starting again. So
                I must decide. Do I get out
                  at Lyon, & take to the
                pissy rides again, can I
              make it to Cannes to
            get back from Cannes.
        Can I make it to water.

Graham knows. The necessary madness.

Wch is a different thing, by sheer will:
the distance to Cannes.
You try jumping
to the moon.
Somewhere,
it is possible.

Im too knackered.
Im not making it
to water & back.
The poem is starting again.
O fuck I cant write it fast enough.
Thru me the way to the city of Dole.
To Dijon.
Lets see what Dijon is.
Am I making a mistake
Im not going to make
the sea.
But all my decisions
are the right one.
Though Im 12 hours
in the truck. I feel like
a girl that wont leave.
& at Dole where we offload,
by a hypermarket, it pisses down,
& for the first time my driver is illtempered.

& now hes heading to Marseilles.
Does he go to Marseilles –
for I shall make the water.

How far will I go.
How far will he go.
It is 4 o clock.
How far will I go.

          & when he stopped at
     a big service station, he sd
he wd sleep, & so I must thank him – whatever is fated. He explains that many lorries stop here & all lorries must go to Avignon, or the garage, where I can get English drivers, Cest no probleme.

I know where Im going. He says he doesnt know why – I can easy get a lorry down to Italy Portugal, Cest tres joli.
But on the other side he says the drivers are 5 to 1 German.
This is the meaning dragging prosody – these barren days

        an end to story:
     & Ive still got 100F
shake his hand I cross to the other service station, looking for milk, cross back to the service station, I cross thru the other service station I dont know, sit on the wooden horse. A dicky bird comes down to me, I goos Tchik tchik tchik & put out my hand to claim him, & it comes & pecks my fucking finger. & for 3 decades this story this notebk this memory the dickybird ended the story

I better do some thumbing w. my cardboard, Vous Allez Paris, w. the copcar checking. Before it gets Iftar.

& stricken w. a relieving of fast wch can hardly be borne: that ravening license

Anyway at 9 or whenever this English bloke in the carpark says hes stopping at the 99F motel wch is all atutomated no front desk, & in the morning hes going to Calais, *But all yve got to do is talk to the lorry drivers any English driverll take y/ but if yre not gone at say midnight then y/ can stay w/ us coz theres noone at the motel it doesnt matter if theres 2 or 3, but as I say y/ shdnt have any problem because this & the other service station a few kms down are the best places, just ask the drivers.*

Is that You, God. Im trying to find you. So anyway the wife suddenly comes from talking to truck drivers & he informs her Ile be staying, then they take me for a Perrier in the cafe, its Iftar, & I leave my bag in thr car & Im thinking theyre drug couriers.

She knows all the drivers from working in her family service cafe. & she says All yve gorra do is talk to the drivers. & then she leaves to talk to the drivers & he says to her, Yeah well dont be long otherwise Ile come looking for you.

& anyway when I go to pick up my bag shes there in the car. & they say Just talk to the drivers theres plenty of British lorries. So I go off to the picnic area to have my bread & Dynamic Body Shaper in the headlights. Excusez moi vous allez Paris monsieur

& later the bloke in the car calls me over & I goos & sit in; & then a pig car comes & naturally wants papers, & as theyre checking Im thinking Im going to be done coz hes a drug dealer, & the wife comes & sits in like a silly cow. I panic theyve fitted something in my bag.

& afterwds I try my halfhearted French on the drivers kipping up for the night, & then me & this kid get talking whos going to Derry or somewhere to live, & we look for drivers together, & I says Ile see if those people will put him up an all. So after midnight I gos to punch the combination at the motel entrance, & knock on thr door

& then the bloke shows me the combination to thr room where his wife is oblivious in thr doublebed & I have the bunkbed. I cant ask about that kid & I go for a shower & forget about it, w. all my stuff rammed in the backback, & my passport rammed in a pocket, & the bag left on a chair & I know someone came creeping in the steam to see what they cd steal.

In the morning I have to get out by the window as the manager or cleaner might find me & then were going to Calais.

& it gets sweltering w. French sun,
                but everything is right.
          He says he was determined
      to give someone a lift when they
    pulled off the ferry at Calais
      to go down to Cote d Azur,
              & do y/ know, I didn't find anyone –
              I was there for 4 hrs.
                  He was where for 4 hrs?
                      I am heere sins I waz born.
                  Im waiting for You, wayting
            for th russle of an heort in dese woods,
      lockt owt da frothing radical certenties
of ða prezent,
I worrie for Yu God,
I worrie for You hwen Im gon

I dont know what theyre up to – maybe they want to use my bag, maybe theyre smuggling *me* –
but we stopped at the next big service station, Bourg or En Bresse, so they can have breakfast, & Ile be wandering around. Take yr bag, he says, in case of coppers; Im like no, but he says, Just take it in case.

& Ive gone for 20 mins to get stamps, & when I come back I cant remember what the car looks like. So Im looking & after a bit it dawns that they got rid of me. So what was that. I still hang around for them for an hour. Looking for You, Allah. Ile wait here just in case its a mistake

At least You left me at the big station, & I know now how to do it. So I make my sign, & the pig car comes round. & standing at the head of the exit, w. the dribbles of cars & lorry, I think How can this not be a good spot.

But you must ask.

At least they left me at the big service. & walking up the lorry lines, a GB trailer pulls away. So there ye go.

I trek up, I trek down. I stand at the bottom & they know Im a vulture. I trek up, I trek down, but you must ask. So I says Excusez moi monsieur – vouz permittez. & track the GB trailers, & the cold comes back.

These coaches & these people, they think Im Wurzel Gummidge lost his submarine; I have come to France to learn to ask: but I am desperate
Hey, dye wanna stop. Cause I am desperate.
I tell y/, there was one line came, w. all the service station grasses & the trees behind a shaking – I was their lord, *I am yr Lord, Ich bin deiner, look on me & laugh.*

I know that all y. have to do is ask the British drivers, they are all cunts, or theyre not yet heading back because its only Wednesday. & when its 6 hrs gone O I am desperate. & when its 7, O I am desperate: standing w. the sign, hunting down the trucks. I was waiting for the owner of this car, & a driver of the GB truck came out, & I sd: Scuse me mate,

there isnt a chance of a lift is there — Im trying to get back to England.
& he hesitates, I cd see he wanted to help — & I told him Id been there
since 12. & he was grieved for me, but he sd he was going to Reims
— & going bk to England tomorrow — I tell you what, it make me
tempted to try & get back; & he was working it out, but he sd Jump
in & well work it out.

  I dont want to leave that warm rumble.
    & I slip into my Brummie, Im showing ye how I belong:
      & I hope he just drives & never sleeps & we make Reims
        in 2 hrs & go on to Calais in the night: wele work it out
        but I am here.

        Thru Dijon hills, the villages, expound
        the bloody fields of two world wars —
     Some people arent interested in it,
   I dont know why — as he points out
   every mound of shells outside
     the churches racing by in twilight
       & I go Mmm.
        The entire time I thght he was
          talking about seashells in Norman walls.
       & for the privilege of this lift Ive got to look at
    memorials & regional differences in war graves.
   I look thru his Klaus Barbie paperback. &
 theres something off
w. his deploring
the wasted lives
in senseless wars.

    Its a beautiful dusk.
      & when we go past
        this cafe in the hollow,

                    he says – Theres a mother
                        & daughter in there,
                            & they say
                    if yre the last
                2 drivers out,
            ye get yr leg over –
        no, true.
    It sounds like a story,
      but I dont think it is.

                I open up the tupperware
                    to make my Dynamic Bodyshaper
                        drink for Iftar, & I neck down this
                            unwashed plastic curdle from days.
                        & he goes Pee-yeew, what is that pong!
                    He has to roll down the windows.

                He keeps arguing whether to fix
            the tacometer for his hours w/out a break –
        (Cest oblige) – & he says Shit, Ile do it.

            Hes helped me out.
                He deserves to go into a poem.
                    This pm nearly over. He reminds of the bloke
                                    in the deodorant advert,
                        who runs outstretched to his Beloved,
                    then sniffs his armpits.
        One last song
      in the palimpsest.
    I shared my nuts w. him.

    One hilly ribboned
        road to the night,

                    past his cemetaries,
                        past a road victim buried
                            on the road.

                    I recognize the kilometres to Reims.
                        & we go in & around it.
                            I dont remember.
                            But I remember
                                the concrete
                                overpasses
                                & pillars
                            dreaming evil.
                        We went down
                    an avenue of lopped or
                stricken tree things,
            fistuled w. switches
                of bare twigs, & all in
                    anthropomorphic horror.

                    O little fortress towns,
                        ane daeg yr werreier elites
                            wil be da veri model of a riot

somewhere in the night he stopped in a layby, & put bk the tacometer & switched off the clock. He was going to sleep till 8 & then wed do the last leg. I was disappointed but, anyway, he squeezes into the cabin bed & I curled up against the door but I cdnt sleep, ye know how it is, in a lorry.

It was cold, & when it was light enough I took this out & started writing. Until he got up again, & still it spitted,
                            & going past all these towns

     & tracts of world war, edging
    up to the great grounds of history.

  Wed be going thru the towns & hed
 be hooting at the women at traffic lights.
I thght there was something wrong.

Yknow I mustve got onto the Gt Sickness – how she gets raped, & I knew there was something off, coz he just goes Tut tut tut. & when I tried to get on the conditioning of people he muses Well, I dont know… Whenever he didnt know hed say, Well I dont know.

& he says, No, I think Thatcher's done a lot of good for this country, she got people off thr backside.

   & when we were past Lille,
    & on the deserted
     crappy National road
      there was blue between
      the white clouds,
     & the sun combed the grass
     in the slick wind.
   & Ile tell you the only song I remember:

 Bimbo Bimbo
  what you gonna do-ee-o
 Bimbo Bimbo
 Where ya gonna go-ee-o
  Bimbo Bimbo
   does yr mother knooow
    that yre walking
   down the road
 w. the little girl-ee-o.

Do ye know what it means?
  I recognized the bastard roads
    of Calais that Id hiked.
      He was telling me about his ex

Unfortunately the wife took my daughter, shes somewhere — how shall I put this — it wd be good for her to know her own culture

In 30 yrs he can wache CBeebiez whare My Storie wil hav Granddad teling his tale to th granddawhter w. a scool photo of him in sume fishing port lik Kirkaldy or Dundee. Al th bonny 50s cildren, & den we see hiz granddochter in th same scool now — de onlie hwite face in da hole class. How th fuk did that happen.

Maybe al th fishermen hav gon to Kerbala or Somaliland to set up fish & chip shops & chapters of th Ku Klux Klan & bred all þe nativs out of sichte.

I hav enormus sympathie for a working oik on da rong syde of da BBC. What can he say about his wife who spirited his girl away. By this stage he was coming off the wall — *That fucking bitch, stupid fucking evil cow, theyre all lying vindictive — facking cunts. Stupid fat facking cow —*

ritten out of da patriarkhi — da mamluks of th new feudal order — tilling somwon elses land to pay fief tribute

do yoo want th lorry driver to die? — repent in a Chineez educacioun camp? — join th Labour party? — join the Intifada? — superglu th toylet seet?

Mate, Ile speke for you.

   At the Calais control,
    I went in w. him: there
     were hitchers at the gate
      looking for a lorry driver:
       I stood in as second driver
        at the Drivers check.
         An 8 & a half stone cupcake.
         & ye dont have to pay.

       We missed the midday ferry.
        Bimbo Bimbo Bimbo…

    ride the plunge of the prow
   meet the rough waves & lace
  the forward windows.
All the English.

Am I the first
  in a Long Vehicle.
    Then follow me crusading coolies!
      swamp th County of Flanders w/ yr blac bodiez,
       wayting for th fishing botes ut of th Dover Straits —
   chaunting *Labbayk, labbayk* —
As we jurney on
we wil sing this sung
for th boooyz in Royal Bleew
weer oooften partizan la la la
*weee wil tu***urn ye on*** *laa laa laa*
keep riht on *to the end* *of th raad*
keep riiht on *too the eend*

He dropped me off at this service station
     between Dover & London

                that sounded out of Sir Gawain.
            & y. know he saved my life.

    So is this the end.
    Because the last bit
    is the hardest.
    As it pissed.
    There I learned
        to ask the drivers.
            & I was still there
                when this bloke who looked like he was still
                    sniffing glue & joyriding, he says Are you lost.
                Turns out he wants to panhandle me!
                His car needed oil bad, & I
                    offered to nick some
                    from the forecourt,
                    but I dont know why
                    I got timid.

            So we get into his sickly bag of nails,
            & we went limping along it was really suffering.
        Were getting to the next service station, & then it went BANG.
    I says That sounded permanent.
He sd, It did, didnt it.
& he starts
effing & blinding.
We roll for 2 miles
    cause the motorway
        was on a downslope,
            & we were going faster
                than when it had an engine.

            Is that a story. I thought it sort of was

a writing that extends sincronuously to past & futur

what
did y. do in Eid:
even the mosque w. Allah
& the trilling of fans, where
I was not

we 28 yr children the unworkabl
makhal of religius feeling –
cult of povertie

who
cdnt be contayned
in Holie Orders
my sister who shd hav been
hustled
aganst her will to a convent to
wail & fret her medieval
fate, but thats exactli
hwat her fate cals
out & then shed hav a shap to her lyf

I cd burn at th words of Stephen
of Cloyes or Stephen burn at myn,
or yoo cd beleve in Tony Benn or
another Holi Fool, & I, a last folower
brocht to Reims or vizionary dawn burn,
buying my passige on merchant ship to be
sold into slavery in Tunis,
onli to fynd th Cildrens Crusade
is also a myth
th way in wch

    my misanthropi
       resembels th Beets
          Lyon —
             didnt my Eestern
                dissolucioun
                    witewash you?

              Oh but where was
                the Joy of landing a bream,
          rushing out of bushes to clamp a Lada,
      oh you dont know — that rush — After long hardship
    & then a kind car out of nothing in my head — **Weeaarrgh.**

I didnt know Rue Frochot was a haunt of Baudelaires. I just found out 30 yrs ago. This is the reason I do it. This never dg it at the time.

Shall I be: the Portable Khaled
& then I got a lift from this kid in a dinky yellow sports car & we were talking about American writers, & he puts me off on the M25.

              & Ile never see them again.

            Qhwat kynd of interloper
          coms mooching up th wolds —
      a peon hoo pays back th empire
      w/ a vayge expectansy he shud be king

Thru me the way into the city of dole
Thru me the way to the eternal deadend
Thru me the way of the shuffling lost soul
who lived w/out infamy & w/out name
a mix of rebel angel & rissole
whose fate is both the pan & flame

                    That double
                              rainbow over Calais,
                                    as today, to write this
                                  seeing the end
                               walking thru
                        villages backward w.
                     yr beauty, laying hands on
        spastic, touching eye & mouth,
seeing the end
a fabulous death
fr a runaway combine harvester

     as it knocks down Constitution Hill
        & the Knife Prow, & knocks down Broad St,
                              & I was too late
                         for my favourite curve
                   in Birmingham the black corner
              rounding from the Grand Hotel & all
         that neo Pugin, wch wd grace my film,
       except too late,
     & I was too late

   Coming round
      on the No. 16 before
         they put up a block of glass.
            & in fog & murk the Nat West sign
               the eye of alien. & now there is no film.

                    Up the stairs, part of the ceiling has collapsed
w. the rain. In the night, a prostitute was trying to break in the
downstairs door. There was a fayre across the road. There was this slip
of an Irish dancer like another world.
But therell never be another story.

Ile tell you how I escape a night of torment w. the relatives. Shall I tell y/ what its like. Why shdnt I make y/ suffer – why not make y/ speak Bangla.

Are yr sisters married.

If I address this to Korean peasants, does it make it all right.

DOLDRUMS – RAMADAN 1987

They sleep with simply.

Whereas you are crotchety. Yeah badtempered. Yes you.

I am badtempered – OK Khaled, I will remember that. I will hurt you so bad, how a condom makes you cry.

You will see my gun, & afterwds nothing.

I will blow yr brains out & say *How I cared for you: Cloudy cloudy all over the wallpaper you will never know how much you mean*

The acrylic accident of a net curtain
is the miracle of this antwing
by deaths strict metre
Deerheart

The boy who threw away his wife –
will he waste his life, all his life

summer w/ fleas & foreign students that makes the liquids inside to shake
who shall be compared to the smell of a cricket ball
but prise out the oysters of yr vulva

The fear of summer:
the lope of ye
w/ a milk in the vision
the cool of water on yr bum

the central round tree twinkles in the way of minnows
Children, where is the nobility. Ye whelps, what does it mean, *Where is the nobility*, even in a spaghetti sci fi film

This conviction of drift

        at 7 the Ikon preview party.
       & at half 8
      Iftar at moms.
     So I get there &
    Pete collars me in the
    acolytes, blind w/out my glasses.
     So what are these big monochromes.

      He drags me downstairs coz apparently
       thats where its at. Photo portraits. Petes manic,
     Im out of it, I mean its hard when yre fasting; & hes
   going Haawww w/ the halfwit aristocritic look at *everything*.
Artist selfportraits thru the ages. Angsty readymades.
Pete gurning the narcissists & running upstairs for drink.

     Swimming w/ yng people. As soon as you write
        'young people' y/
        know what I think.
         For my days are like
         a shadow that declineth;
         &I am withered like grass
       Are they famous in the shade.
      Ye can feel it doesn't sing – does it
   reveal a shoddy charlatanism w/ no structure
   waiting for 8.35;
  while Pete is going *Kkrrrsshh krrgwrsh – O-keey*:
& then giving me his *Im gonna start* look.

             Its no use. Its Ramadan.
                  I love it walking past Theory –
                       its got no relation to a tight bra.
                            I wont be making Iftar.
                         Are you Steve, yre Steve.
                            No *Im* Steve.
                        Hes Steve. Whos this Steve.
                 & Im out of it.
         The circulation of authority
       in a thousand peer reviews –
    circulating downstairs & in a fatman photo:
    another Steve,
       the Steve,
          a Steve,
                another artist
                     naked at his piano,
                          & Pete w/ a Jimmy Durante paper cup nose.
                            I wonder if there are any artists here.
                              They shall look back on the
                                   prodigious rush
                                 & call it macaroni.

                              Getting to Iftar
                       when I cd be foaming & cracking
                    like Pete accosting acolytes & thr boyfriends.
                  Hey wheres the next Iftar. Theres always a next Iftar.
           She says, I am. But I know:

My apple juice time.

My marionette Pete, his shadow who says that all the eyes began to close as the exhibition went on.

That lonely girl who looks like Mary Shelly at the magazines.

Yknow, when I sd at 9 that I want to push off for moms & eat, Pete gets all earnest & insists *Im alive*.

Were reading the w/drawal of funding from the Triangle in WM Arts Report. So maybe theyll never ask for the £100 I owe.

These reticences damage you.

We go out to look for Pete whos disappeared, & me sick w/ fruit juice

Ah help, help the fool yr son
w/ the eyelashes of llamas
with my lemon & sweet girl
with my lemon & sweet God

There was that sick inside & the olive in the skin:
much love much love

so when Pete gets bk, & everyones leaving: & hes not letting up the antic posture & eyeballing;
I better go its too late. Ile have to stay at Moms & watch Joan Collins. & then Pete will do his obeisance.

Hed had to get out, nearly in a scrap w/ someone. This big bloke eyeballs me as I leave & shoulders me. Is that Steve.

Dont you think Im naive. Theyre not difficult. They tremble like popcorn.

Lets go to Soho Rd – we wanna go somewhere the Vietnamese grannies wear peasant hats & babies.

So we go to the theatre pub. Stuffed w/ the Ikonites & Steves & Yng People. Why isnt it over – I want it over.

I better buy Pete a drink. People still want to twat him for his Gestapo coat. Im glad this isnt a pm: because for the next half hr Pete is asking for it, & this bloke thinks were a double act in the history of fatuity w/ a cigarette up his nose

Are you Steve. No shes Steve.
Steve is not a Substance. He is a state of mind.

How we weep for this shirt. How we weep for nothing.

A not real Steve making commercial nose casts & finding funding; a manly Steve making sandcastles

Theres Pete in the corner w/ a woman. So we ambush him – *Fock off*. Yknow, that bloke goes by & *looks* at me. Its daunting to be w/ someone more aggressive than me.

When I ought to leave, to eat, Pete is adamant Im an Interesting Guy. Otherwise, while hes snogging that girl at the bar, I feel his leg, & then start feeling up the girl as his extra hand.

& then when we look back hes in an altercation over a spilt drink & I go in to keepem apart – Yewanna nut me, go on then – & the bloke says Id need a step ladder

& the girl *rushes* to look uninvolved

But were out, though I must eat.

& I try to trip up Pete, he gets me in a headlock & throws me to the pavement & starts crushing my jaw.

I leave y/ there, not to be published either, to break fast at Moms, the flagrant rainbow, w. its 7 league feet over Cotteridge, who knew that the wld is so small

Run with bellyache a way scattered w. blossoms

a melding moon almost talking
& then imagine breaking fast with a clean stone the cold of evening in a borrowed coat: & the cold of water in the cold.
What did you do, what did you do
so broken, to expatiate all my fathers, & run, from mom, that if only the body wd take over, become a trance figure seeing the pavement tipping me home w. a catch in the eye

you sombre dick

what do we seek, a convulsive extraversion of a hairy old bum
in the readerless placeless lostness

Again. Again, the same poem
how many giro chqs get stolen in the same poem

Refrain: refrain refrain refrain

A flaccid pulse:
the entire body of aphasia is this regret

Saqi, Ile tell y/ mortificacioun when th batterd cild next door mimicks
my rage thru th wall

gimme another englyion coz nothing helps

eche ane of y/ who byes this book helps me fynde my place
help me fynde my plac yoo panders – thers a plac hwere th hero maks
hire way down th duodenum hwer simply dozens of th benign elect
feel th same way as th masses

but I know, I know there must be thousands

a pact w. God to kill yrself as slowly as He wills

Meanwhile back in Heaven things are hotting up alright

This text that cries just like you, when you feel like this
These things are broken on my mind as toothpaste.

Find yr place, poet, a bourgeois in the black economy

TO THE HITCHHIKING DEAD 1987?
– (NEW YORK?)

as we waddle into the sunset
my sisters, I must burn it out, &
the journey into endless night, &
the pact w/ things you fear bigger
than a sisters paper cut, a sisters
tiny invisible eyes,
now y. forget the violet
& the orange tinges coming
down on road flats:
& so, the meaning coward
must expel y. into the strangest pm,
because the biggest fear is the familial myth,
the personal excuse that buries theogony in yr crap

I dont knwo what the smell is in yr traces, the toasted cream cheese
to expunge – trying to say it just once so its sd forever

reams of this, reams of lust,
people running to the saddest rust,
people running to the summer *mast* –
summerblown to the endless dust

to say it just once: this twilight section,
this hermetic or iterative groove, this
dislocated self, a sausage machine
for incestuous silence
the Gt Work as neurotic disguise,
when for people dead like us, we can think

of the endless children, I only can love me when
      I hear me sob so sweet,
         gee, yve got such
            aristrocratic eyes,
         even when theyre filled
      w. rheum
      walking off into the endless rhymes –
     O Susan Hayward – trace over the memories!
    only dont give us that goo

   th pages seem to cleve three divergent jottings –
an fliȝte to NY wircan van deliveriz for my *mamas* now lost
theez words, hoos direciouns ar now lost

& for the first time the devil ran out,
  & his muscles hurt, what did he do in the night,
    did he run around after iftar, w/ all those hot little Hispanics
   I dont know, the saga doesnt say

     oh quickly finish my song –
     the nightmare of the one
     supramundane surge
    of passion –
   as the character
  gets bogged down w/ old reruns
as I escape as 18th C noble somewhere in Europe
to take bk the pattern of thr regressive Grand Tour
O SING for the first time the pm forever talking at the edges of its legend

   a journey
     beginning w/ effacement
       w/ the U boat captains cap,

                    already washed up on the edge of tragic
                he had a cadillac in his left eye (R. Johnson)
             travelling 2 months w. the hindsight of what yre
       dying of,
    before y. realize
yre dying fr the travelling

This Austrian kid, he was only 17,
he sd, Gd bye mother, because the way Im going,
like everybodys talking to me 2 yrs ago, or theyre already
   dead.
   Im going for love,
        or Im going to die,
             either way its death.

                the silver sword can use the water
                   in one great burst of florescence,
                & then dies

          if y/ drain every gd wd for th pm –
      this is the infantil undertaking in
    letters,
   so in the absens of ptry or brain cells
   the task of looking for the compatible
      gene like looking for her footprint
      in a thousand mile marathon
       a radical brakthru of form
                into Haqq –
                  wich
                looks lic a
           digestif bisqit & cup of PG Tips –
        for steorvende man an absolut & sayntly appearans

77

along a seafront tide in, the same prospect of the little Venetian
humpbacked bridge far out in the wavelets w. black seals crawling &
sliding off. There is enough discrepency & 15th C perspective to be
authentic. Out in the sea blk seal heads bobbing. A hoary old polar bear
heaves in & ploughs into them:

the herpes ridden shoals & raggedy predator.

        I a schilling soldier in the SS,
      in yr kitchen like the Sylvester party;
     in the border barracks we must jump onto
    the elevated arm of the checkpt barrier. Every
   time I leap the barrier lowers. Its not my fault
  I cant do allocated duties: the duty officer
  must take the blame. The Kommandant
 & soldiers enter the buro: he is cowered
in the corner stammering. They put his hd
& shlders into a kind of brace, a tourniquet
w. large splint beams down his body. He is under
lights & the big executioner get his neck & the halter
          is tightened.

I am a gd Nazi, just trying to follow orders.

this is the tragedie in wch we cleve –
th pull to separacion & th pull to herd,
an imaj of mate that makeþ hale, the urj to
Bavarian stock,
      out of this moment
       of malnorished shic,
      ut of anxietie to bigger dik
     in yoo, clowdy allure, th call to be normal
    in this, my commodifid imperatif
   to be a crippeled elite

O orenge tanned siren,
in 30 yrs I cannot forget
yr Terrible truth –
Yre not too big,
yre not too small –
yre juuust riht.

DOLDRUMS 2020 – 2007 – 1987

Last nichte I betraiyed you
now I cume to bow
last niht I betrayed eow
& th dead com back to vow
Yoo ar th One, yoo are the anly one

last ni3ht I prayed for you
my hert ane ball of fyre
last niht I draggd yu down
& now Ive cume to crawl

I MADE A VOW TO YOO
I MADE A VOW TO YOO
& I WENT BK, I WENT BK
I DONT CNAW HWIYE DO
I DONT CNAW HWIYE DO
& YOO COME BK, YOU COME BK
YOO AR ÞE ONE, YOU AR THE ANLI ONE

Hay Allah
this bag of nonsenss kneels down to you & sends his longing & luve
may this handful of luve
be all th lov I need
Hay Allah – you mad this creture & w/ yr help, You can unmake him

thire ar so many ways to die, living untill yre dead is ane,
getting th boies to finish thir brekfast is anoðer,
dying w/ yr unborn cild is th last
ðeres ane tiny pilot licht in th boiler

& it used to be Yr heort lichting th way to Hades
hwer am I Deaþ, its 2020 & I havent been payd yet

O Darling yre calling me bac,
bac to th bed th boi th donkey & th pack
bk to the protectorat attick & th rack
a madman blinded by th governess for luve

But for You – I wd drown in a dezert
but for You – I wd parch in a lac
You hav a voyce
& I am yor tunge –
dragging acros th sands
for a taste of you –
Hak Dost!

Labbayk, labbayk, do as you will
I am yr puppet & I am yr glove
I am yr slap & I am yr love
mor than an engel & less than a dog

Labbayk, labbayk
I am yr proof, & I am yr siʒne
I am yr *ghulam* & you ar myn
kill me ones morr, bræð lyf into me
for I am endleasly þyn

Oh shit – Im bk in England.
Oh shit – Im bk in NY

The butterflies rushed in coming thru the underground corridors, to
Arrivals. If y. cd meet on that rush.

In a month he was a failure on a coach looking for *Dost* one & a half hrs late, & spilled milk over his neighbour. He wanted to go into her arms, His arms, anyones arms, saying Im soooo sorry Im late.
A girl that is waiting in Charing X, a girl waiting in Victoria, w/ no second class chances.

The wds that became important were: doch, peepul, kitzlich, maybe…

At Piccadilly Circus, Khandan, the night bus, Khandan, the night bus pulling away, & first I jump on, & y/ Khandan, if it was you, *beti*, dont know the gear changes, wrenching yr grip off the bk pole, as y/ fell back into the street dwindling. If it was y/ Khandan, instd of schlumfen *beti*.

Ohh, my leg, she sd, poor B. in London.
She stayed crumpled on the kerb. I am so schlumpfen, all year I have accident, schlumpfen B.
A was chiding himself, I feel so bad Ray.
Its nothing, they sd, as she got up the bus stairs, as they amputated her leg. The busride black & beautiful, veered between dream church squares & Georgian corners, illuminated in footlights.
I feel so bad, he sd.
Two tender crutches.

On the train she sd she must always cycle once in the day to Bregenz to see the peepul; she always must want to meet w. interesting peepul. Always she finds shwein, but always she finds an expression in thr face, that makes them interesting.

It was my last chance to be a loser. Some kynd of lonly pantherus dragging a deor into bushes liccing its papps.

I have – a list, in my mind, of all the interesting peepul, I must meet –
& I know that I will meet this person. & when I have met this person I
put a cross I put a tick against this person. & one day my list will be full.

I must face it (100 x)

Come into this flat, floral disinfected. Eat these Indian tidbits. Sleep w.
my forearm barring yr chest. A pantherus alreddy extinct.

He had come bk – I – *I* had come bk from NY. Oh no, I came bk from
NY! So nervous, so sick & nervous. Again.
What is it *beti*, are y. going bk.
The adult Downs locked out in the hallways moaning & braying,
Myomma, momm, shuffling downstairs crying & angry, the distant cop
car, its all so dangerous
What is it.
& shell trickle some more, touching his collarbone:
I think, I must go bk.

At times a numbing fear comes over me in the courtroom; at other
times everything seems pointless, a ticket for the laundry. I want to
scream out at the traffic lights, Dont y. understand, someones trying to
kill me!

While he was watching the cricket he fell out of love.

DOLDRUMS 1987

some people think Yoga is flower arranging
Ive come bk fr karate w. ballooned up hands, lumps on forearms,
busted toes, chest & arms in spasms: but I wd never do Yoga
Now Im going up town to get some money.
Dont ask about my party.
Bakr is locked out of Brians
If life follows a story, then it follows a pm.
He has to wait till 6, walking round Handsworth.

At midnight the buzzer goes & I put on my hat. Its the French sounding bloke: I invite him in & hes being apologetic & I suddenly understand he needs a place for the night. So Im in my kitchen he goes into his story cause hes a writer too. & Tunisian! Doing commercial photography in Paris; hes going on about his aimless migrations, that ended in his illegal overstay here. I like him but his eyes are like a rodents. & the difficulty of getting US visa or work in France or Germany. & hes got paintings in Amercia – did he mention he was a painter as well. Oh, I thght, he doesnt really do anything.

O I cd go on w. this story, he just wants to sleep on the rug w. a piece of canvas as a coverlet; talking about his filmscripts & 2 expensive 16mm shorts, he knows hes got to do a real film in his life; just give him 6 months. Oh yes, I talked too.

Now its half 2, still obsessing about my ex. Exs seem to stand as prohibited kin, not good to fantasize on

a transparent larva the size of a fingernail at the edge of predation

The white trail of a plane drifting in altitudes,
in the icy meridian w. a plum dusk coming
down.

Rather than forge home,
there is too much seeking thru
the valley of aridity.
This pm is written for
other children who need
a protector of the road.

The centreless journey
an irresistible archetype,
& its centred too.
Its not meant for those
whove done nothing hardier
than campus. Its like a big fat honorary
cat going off to mortifications as instructed

To the beggars, to the shanty towns,
I hope you get this book, I hope
you get enough to eat, & I wish
yr families health. The future has
daw3ters
taw3ht forto breac & parents ground down
wif justiss tho3h writen on tablets for God,
& sons who pled þe lack of 40000 witnesses

Wære ar You Perfect Khaliq,
þat plases such Divine Names in
an animals brest, a hopeless cærless brust –
Ya Adl Ya Muqsit Ya Adl Ya Musqsit wif all the
unforgiving peine & need for haeling of a wolfpack,
a socialy bound Dæmon

there are tears & there are tears,
hold bk the audience in the riant fictions
all the trees are green tears given to the wretch next door
She takes it out on the kid. I take it out on her. & we get along:
Give it a rest. Give it **a rest** willya!
Knock! Knock! Knock!
spk in tongues w. the wall
keep vigil till dizzy
(knock, knock, knock)

& *Beti* gave me this frosty letter...
but in the evening all the figures in the dark
on the school green suggest theyre going to have
                                      thr Diwali bonfire.
                    So Bubakr shows me his crappy art.
              Well, in some way, certain parts
      of the painting can be almost
 worthless.
They start to make a stage...
Its almost not there. Its just something to put the words on.
& then they light the bonfire so out out out w. my second string
nonreflex Bolex & a packet of letters my love.

They go up
  in the offering incens,
     O Kaiserling herzling,
        th fat of yr letters curling up
            to adolesent Gods, w. *Beti* & Samantha,
                thr adeqwat meeger oblaciouns to me – my sacrifyce!
                    even tha letter þat yu pasted a peece of carpet.
                        Shed glewd a furry hart she cut out from
                            th back of her cat. & some smartass
                                onlooker crooning – *Oh baby,*
                                  I cant beleeve its oveerrrr...

Can anyone make use of so many conjunctions & still
       be an artist.

        this poem
    is addressed to you illiterate poor –
  I dont mean unemployed fitters in Lowestoft
  y. wont understand that saying it is the container
   but its addressed to you & there are things y.
    can understand, like *bhat* & *shutki shirra*
     for brkfast, & anyway y. havent
       got much choice.

      & its the poem
    where I burn the past again
   & the shots of the Catherine Wheel
       & candle mantras

I gave up the Bolex to the local blk gang & Bakr gets knocked out. & a couple of neighbours open the door. *Are those the lads – Oh I know them, they live around here.* Then they come bk & one of them takes dudgeon Im still hanging around & goos Bang in my jaw, Im picking up my hat & she says *You can come in if y. like love.* I says Are you talking to me, & she says *No, Im talking to him.*

What are they touring in the copcar for w/ Bakr
but we learn this is probably the 3rd mugging by this lot

The story cd contain the shooting of the bonfire on my Bolex watched by the gang, or sussing them run past in the school entry, or letting the case go like Gandhi. Or the police statement in the flat; but we shd get to the one real story when theyve gone, & Ive justified myself.

Bubakr was w. his girlfnd in Tunisia & they were walking the beach at night nowhere to lie but feeling gd, & hed noticed a group of bikes following & then theyd disappeared, so he guessed they were lying up somewhere – I asked how many, & he sd 7.

& the one sd We want the girl: B reasoned w. them shes Swiss & European & if anythg happens to her yre cooked man, the authorities will find y. & execute y.

So they say – We fuck the girl, or we fuck you. *When I hear that, I just go Taaash like that – in his balls, & he goes down & I just get on him & Im hitting his face, like this, on the metal grating, & I sd to Nicole, Quick, first on the right & then left – Ile meet y. there.*

What were the others dg – *Oh they were around, yknow, kicking me, like this – but when Im like that I dont care – I just want to kill him. Yknow one of them pick up this Big Stone, big as yr amplifier, & they go like that – & it just go past my shlder & I just say, Hey, y. shdnt do that. So when I see Nicole is safe I say to them, Hey look, the police are gonna be here, y. better be gone.*

So he tells his brother the Family Strangler, & the guy comes crawling round to call him off – but thats Tunisia. When 7 men want to fuck you y. can say plainly: where parts of a pm can be almost worthless, theyve earned thr worthlessness, & others thr purpleness. Its just somethg to put the wds on. A piece of art thats no longer there.

But he was never able to get it on w. her after that – he tried, when he went to Paris & they were gd fnds, but there was somethg between them. Im forgetting this isnt mine, but I havent got any stories like that. In the Paris Metro, when he passed 4 skinhds writing immigrant lyrics on the wall, & they turned to him & sd *You dont like it* – & he sd No I dont like it. So, for one minute, we kicked each other. We just kicked for one minute. & then they carried on w. thr graffiti & he went on waiting for a train.

Ive got stories like his other story where hes w. a gdlooking girl on the Metro & 2 Algerians come & bother them & then one of them knocks him out. He shd have called the skinhds.

Oh yeah, when the blk kids chase him up the school alley, he was always conscious of the one w. the knife, the one standing behind me, & he put too much pace & tripped, & they jumped on him. There were people around & noone helped Tchaa –

Because karate-do is nothing less than coming to terms w. existence in the rugged theatre of the Dojo

the wind w. ghostly harmonies keening thru the camera scaffolding on a Hawaian golf course

How desperately a pm
    can grab the case & run
        after real being, fling the
            reflection of fire in car glass
                Bakrs story wd be that Id be
                    knocked down in happiness

            I had no possibility of not bg you.
            You had no possibility of not bg you.
          But when I was put into song, instantly
        in the mouth
    sayer & sd remove fr embarrassment
I in spiritual quest in pms impossibly, deservedly unfashionable

But what has anythg got to do w. weeing in yr pants, how can y. be so menopausal, living in a multicultural area, Ive been attacked by a variety of multicultural people.

Terror gripped a Holiday island, as a wild child carrying the AIDS virus
infected dozens of public schoolboys & local fishermen
& we can reveal the name of the beauty is French girl
Anastasia Helvig, 18

O my God, y. pissed in yr pants, FUCK they were only just washed &
smelled of 4 days drying in the bathroom.
Oh my God, Ive still got to finalize the script read thru & schedule the
dry run.

A Buddhist prayer gong rings symbolic representations:
Im w. the Spies
Brian declares himself v. tranquil, trumpeting tranquil farts. Brian
farted thru the night & got more tranquil. Steve declared feelings of
tranquillity were arising. It was too cold to sleep & the blankets were
hairy & dusty.

I admire thr chanting in the morning. The *Gohonga* another instrument
of Utopian rule. Brian continues farting.
We go off for a jumble sale, for clothes some father might have died in.
Brian finds a round collar shirt & kipper tie that begins the first of the
portents
a fictive waffle to invoke enigma – everything is holy in yr hagiography
feel the stresses in the jerrybuild
I was at a Hannah Wiener reading in St Marks – from forgotten
journals transcribing her restructuring her molecules thru strawberry
jam & the karma of star signs. They sd, Well shes been ill for a long
time. Hey, *Ive* been ill for a long time! But I heard her mutter it was
the worst thing shed ever written.
The first portent is not feeling desperate. The second portent is Brian
lost my trousers. Were sitting in the pub Brian blinking proudly in his

Bollywd quiz show gear, a performing village idiot as healthy as it gets for a schizophrenic. I am proud of my village idiots.

I have lost 2 hrs like the Boston Strangler.

The blokes across the street chuck a brick at the transvestite shop & I realize it cd get worse
the same nuttiness of Catholic ritual, the same nuttiness in Marxist hoovering of morals into God the Leveller, same sympathetic magic God bless thr little Hegelian hearts

On Gibson Rd, 3 blk kids are coming up, & 2 block the road, but Im turning up the rd. Because this is 8 or 9 portents, I scare myself silly brushing rattling hedges, I think I see them follow, then I do hear running coming up, & I pretend the first garden path is mine & swing in as a blk kid pounds past in a ski mask.
Fuck its the same mugger!
The 9th portent is still possible
A toy clock somewhere chimes 12.
Snow fell.
A pm written in exorcism.
The books being read were: Narrative as Performance (Marie Maclean); The L=A=N=G=U=A=G=E Book; Sleeping With Plastic (Kenneth Koch); I am a Total Wanker (Pablo Neruda)

TO THE HITCHHIKING DEAD 1988 – LANDS END

   you strings of spermatoza
in hot bath water
  more fantastical than ever
    waiting for the right folksong
       to inspire the pineal organ
         on top of my brain

       make like a leaf child
  waiting for the season of
gonadotropic hormones
in the starling calendar
   at once to urge migration
     & stimulate my milk
      O Proclavin, proclavin
         keep me here paternal *gharial*
           keep me here infernal ariel
             keep me in the eternal unreal

       Just for a minute feel the gurgle up yr shins
      Have a look at the sun. No really.
    I still dont understand God, but are we going thru pink
      scaffolding & the hiss & shocks of worksites dripping in
        Needless Alley
          the pm a gun mike past terrific bus brakes
         I heard them in the Body Shop
          I heard them in the Body Shop
        but God helps my mascara run

             Ah, you beautiful lowbrow –
            ah you 2nd person pronoun,
       yle always be urging against the limits
    scientist words do stand in the desert of the soul –
    but they must spk of thgs unseen by poets or farmers
         but if everybody in the wld keeps chickening out

           having been the spermbank, he is not allowed the father
              Id like to buttonhole you in the commodity
                who bought books because roughly
                     the shape of a telly

                   I dreamed I went to Bham
                   as I was going to Bham –
                   Union St & Carr La, all
                    the streets Id shoplift –
                  so coming into town, I cd cry
                   at the light of the upper salesrooms –
                     as this glass front of a winebar cut fr
                        the bkground blue & BT tower,
                          wch moves
                             because one of us moves

                        we yng lions, moved on
                         by prides of females,
                      more like dispersed seeds,
                   more important to keep moving
             & after 2 wks mate every 15 minutes

    sumetyms y/ just need a plase name –
                                                    Lands End –
                                          everi region has a Lands End,

        & somwaere a steorving postman
       or a cat dying in a dicch is thinking,
          I must get to Paradis Sircus

Everything the foot touches will be kissed

  as a Man With No Notebook leaves his mom
  & gets off the no 11 & walks down midnight
Hamstead Rd distraught he must leave
familiar things, & even the cemetary woods
  w. its petrified maw of Mara is sorry to see him go.

  I can never cach up w. this fugitif to say, Itll be all richt,
     wele see y/ later, hurry up & drop yr balls. He is Th Man
                                W/ut a Notebk.
                    A lost poet in another centurie,
              refuzing poetri as a subsitut for lyfe.
     & a steorving cat sets ut from Heethfield Rd w.
  a sleeping bag in a bag, to land at Lands End.

    O baby loon, I luve yu so, when yu pack
    yr flannel & walk owt th door, to a sliprode
      in Sandwel or Graet Barr, & y/ kisst my face
        on a lonly iyland

       Hoo gnows how y/ got to Bodmin Moor.
        Dere was an Austin Morris van to Exeter
          or Exmuth – *Go to Faalmuth,* he sez –
            plenti of fanny in Faalmuth. I think he
              was Fred West. Yers later I realiz,
              he cd be Fred West driving
            from Glowster. & I cd catch
        up w. this fugitif to say, *Itll be okay.*

He wont kill yu.
Thurs plenti of fanny in Faalmuth.

O babe, hwen y/ wawk owt that door, w/
a 5 inch blade in yr lunchbox, pleze dont go,
dont g**OO-OO**aaoh,
Im taking 10 steps closer
wen y/ walk owt that door

Holy crap, Stephen reminds me I got pickt up by that genteel woman off th iyland – didnt she drop off twa hangdog drifters alongside – probbly pissd off I ruind thir chanse to rob her. She seemd to pick up a lot of hicchers from that iyland.

Anyway, she let me stay in her Cheltenham haus, & I must hav askd her if she ever had second thowts bringing peeple in, but she tho3t th best of poeple, Just treet them as theyd lyk to be treted, she miyht hav sd. Typical Cristian pinko.

& anyway in th morning hwil she gav me brekfast I sd I wanted to giv her sumthing but all I had was a muffin. She sez Pass it on. I sd I feel th need to giv y/ th muffin. She seyz Pass it on.

It has been my mission to pass on th muffin.

Fuck now I remember leving Handswirth way too late. It was lik 4 o clock, I thght I was mental setting ut then, wat th fuck was I dooing al day –

    & hwat was I doing at the iyland
        al morning wen she drops me off.
            It was suppost to be a good plas.
            I supose it was won scratchy lift
        tacking to another al th way down

    to Somerset or Wiltshir. In the
   passenger seet of late summer
   w/ sume ethereal driver
   & he sez Ile say sumthing
   þat may shock yu –
    wen I haf these phisical
     distraciouns I masturbate
      so I can concentrat on
       higher þings.
      Hwilch
    Ile agree,
   apart from
  the higher.
Cuz I never
 got anyware near
  Cornwal bifore dark.

   Sume driver sd,
     Dont get cawht at Bodmin Moor – evil plase.

        He is taking a cattel trane
         to his mom, & stranded in
          th nicht at Bodmin Moor,
       trying to walk down cuntrie
       rodes w/ a thumm stuck out, w/
      th fog cuming down,
     a fog from Scooby Doo,
     a fog from *Th Fog,*
     a fog waer th Beeste
    of Bodmin creeps
     to mate w/ Cornish cats

                I coont see my feet on th kerb,
                    I cudnt see th kerb, w/ th will o th wisp
                        heodliyhtes softly creeping, w/ th cars
                            softly creeping bottom gear in th fog
                        till they brush past th silouett of a post-
                    man or a ships captin w/ his thumm owt

        The fog swirling & I put my hand ut & I
    coont see my hand. I had to stand stock
    still not gnowing
    hwear th rade was, trusting þoz cars
        wd slyd by w/ thir foglichts twa feet away
                never gnowing I was ðere –

                    5 minits later th fog rols behind me
                            past th cuntrie cotages & ut in front is
                        th crispy furrows of ða moor, & th rodeside
                    trees ar glæming hard & th cotage liʒtes hard;

        & ut on th moor a fat hwit churn of dogh cumes roling,
    it rols down
    th shaggy moor
        to th bondary wall,
            & over lic sæ scum,
                & creeping acros th raad,
                & Im bethinkend ðis is probly an optical iluzion,
    it looks lic wall but it wil be difusse. But it creeps up lic alien ooze up
    to misschif, swalows my feet, swalows my heed, & th hard cuntrisyde
    is gonn, & cars ar gan softly creeping hame.

    It rols away, th hard khroma of cuntrisyde rade under artificial liʒt
    cumes bac, th hwit surf rolls in on th moor. & hwen thers a braek in
    th fog for th 5th or th 10th tyme, I walk dan & find th first radsyde

cottige w/ a secluded porch, & I tak owt my sleeping bag & pray þey
never open da front door as I doss dan on th marbel

      th way Ile cume
     in 20 yeres, & scrabbel at yr porch,
    hyding in King Markos castel fr th dog
    curld up utsyde – & I cannot fynde y/
    I cannot fynd Yoo – th ball of twyne
     is in my heod, but th way erazed
      & þey bilt ten thuzand
       storige sheds
     to line my maze

   cume
  into this shed
  sad Khandan, cume
   into this sleeping bag
    my ded *beta*, & cume into
     this sleeping bag Mad Grayham,
      & cume into this sleeping bag my
       Clement *qadr*, you cant hurry fate,
      she gnows how to wayt,
      O my suffering punishing *beti*,
     her tears ar yor confetti
    cume into this sleeping bag –
   I dont gnow whoze it is –
  but God is in it – yr Frend,
 yr sufering punishing end
yr asses milk & adder
Hes a soft, rich
tea bisscit
on a cold
marbel
grund

Thru that sleeping bag thru my mac, thru my layers, that marbel seeps, & that fog seeps in. & sumetyme in th nicht a car turns in on th gravel, th lihts go ronde th cottige to th bac, & I heare them cume in th bac door, & then a mad scrabbling on th bær floor insyde, I heare th dogge cume scrabbling – me beþinkende I hope dis thing cant smell me, but of cours it cumes yapping & scracching at the other syde of th door.

Al this tym Im thinking I hope nowone opens th door & finds me – theyl haf to moove me on or invite me in, but they cant leve me heer, I just want them to leve me heere. Oooh, let my haire be washt in dust & her chin abraded fr brisstles

  Ooo-ah cold was the grund, dark was th Lord,
    dark as th fog that cam into my shrowd
     dark as th clowd of lye
      Yr wifman lays on me
    deres a bottelneck slide trembling in stars,
  & He sez Oo-oawaa oh-mmmmaaah aah,
 & I dont want to shair him,
 I dont want to shar wif da ni3te
or th blinded stars,
not his blacness,
not his blindnes,
not infirmness,
but his slavish luve for Þu
broken on a hweel of dharma,
that he becumeth unbaerabel swete,
Oh Allah, let me not be broken so luvablie to Yu,
let nat moðer ne myn sistren be so luvabel to Thee, lyk
Yu luvd my cuzen, let Þyn wif & childer be ere so caerfree,
let us be as irredeemably incompleet as beares dispaire

save me Lord for sum nonsens in th futur, th shap of a notbook
soked in th Profhet, a protectif schield of Ribena dat remynds y/
Yoo ar not you

I can never be free of yow
                      Allah,
           & Yu are not yet free of me –
      yow cd have hid me in da flaming sap
   of Ari Upp,
                 ane dryas shynyng wif al th
    drugs of ðe animal kingdom, da wildnesse
   of a 6 yr old in a 15 yr old bodi
     I cd haf been a mulatto slav in Tenasee
         hoo joynd a Minstrel show to
             hyd hisself in Blacfase

Dere Allah, did y/ give me a brain tumor – Ile haf to stir testosteron
into plaster of Paris

Ooo leve me to sleep, lefe me w/out a noteboc pretending Im on-lif.
& I heare the dochter telling th dog at th door to shush, & finaly
th mann cumes to drag tha dog at my eare away.

Sleeping w. another mans unwritten ptry
this feeling of always having been in it
now put in the dreary fantastical:
a classrom, a stage, a stadium
a jungle w. human botflies
the mosquito nets of
yr own making

the same journey
in strange cars running

deserted roads in walled up
mazes; burnt on the retina a Shangri La
of Yugoslavia, a beach of rock-pools w. rocks,
of dunes w. water, & a shelf dropping to applegreen tides
a dream of dawn burn, in a sexuagenarian doze
a fever of brokenness clouded thru years

I never cd get warm.

Lands End is not Lands End.

        & after Lands End,
          ther is a trek or 3 mile ryde,
            to be staring at the ecge of th
              sunny gnown wirld w/ all
                th picnickers.
                 & lic Mont Everest,
                y/ hang abot for
               15 minits w/
              yr mac folded up,
           & too litel ayre to go rownd,
        & dicide its tym to go bac.

    I got 6 rides to go 12 miles.
I cd have gone quicker on rollerskates.
a convoy of refugees
  escaping a hippy festival in Basra
    & in no particuler impaciens.
      Evry ride ends at th next villij fork.
       & my plase cells end heere

         the head of a collie sticking out
        of a broken pane in a pub
       & other literary precedents

        & so I was dropped off
      before midnight
    on the M42 to Coventry,
     hreowing ðis flyover
       & immediately this Luton van
          w. 3 in front spins round the colums & pulls up,
            & I braced myself for trouble as I trudge up
              & Paul sticks his head out past the others & says,
                Sister Raaay. I thght it was you. Fucking ell.
              They just cume fr a gig.
          So this is the pm:
        sitting in the pitchdark
     w/ thr band equipment,
  rocking w. the flashes
of orange motorway
streaking over the tarpaulin & my craziness, heading somewhere Birmingham

did they drop me Digbeth?

as poets, who by wanting everything,
  get nothing, but this is about so much,
          God – its so loose, so loose
     as a prince comes blinking out of
      the harem into rule

        So give it to me Poeisis:
          the negative ptics of realism –
            its out there, there is something
              worthwhile, there is there,
            as well as here.
              Ile shape y/ God,
                Ile shap You a God,

                    a seeking speking
                  parasthetick presshur
                or temparatur or magnetizm
           If y/ strip it all out, if y/ shear th coyls
         of His locks, tangld in yr braciats
       strip al the acsidents of artifis,
      & leve a Godshapt mute
      a mening w/ a si3ne
     pms so terrible
      there are no wds for it
        a terrible thing when she
          is now the rolling stone
             & only coming against night
              wind railings
                 youve waked thru the cemetary elms –
                  use that walks analogous shadows –
                O use me,
              take me w/ y/ when ye go
           lose þis boc & lose yrself
       Tell them to folow yr voyce
    Ari Upp,
  O tel them th qwicsand is calling,
 tel them to danse to the end of my lash
  deeth is irritating gas
   y/ ar my Habibti,
       & if that sonds tuched, remember
          its a long tym sins God was publishd
            hoo showed y/ how to be a mænad
             w/ut selfharming?
              hwa tawht y/
           th way of th blac bottom running slav?
taste the swamp running down yr spine
Holy Roman Empire in decline

kiss me quick Caligula
meet me underneath the pier
call an orgy for the fish
call an orgy for the dish
slipping & sliding
all the lambs jump in frying pans
they sizzle w/ mint sauce
sizzle w/ mint sauce
lie down in the oil
lie down in the moil
put yr pebbles in my mouth
slipping & sliding
to be yr feral bkward son
a grunting wolfboi of Hesse
utterli fukt by th Sorbonn
Leve me on th Fowndling steps, messieur Roosoaw sir
thats al richt, Ile die slowly in thir tender care,
yoo go off & tel th wirld how to look after me, teche them th root of all evil is Enlihtenment
usher in the age of Pol Pottery, of overagd cildren on student lones
speking sooth to Whitey

AaarRRRGH cume bk Khaled, cume bk, its all unreal,
these word pernicketing dingoes
because God has been kind w. them, I am unkind to them
& hoo wil be kynde to my lorrie driver…

hwat da hell did I eate?

DOLDRUMS 1988

All the cars driving backwds in the world, 26.II.88 moves to the only future. Transmuted into Limbo.

Stay thire in innosent tymes, waere the occasional outrage aganst a lowcaste cild hwo steps utside unchaperoned is offset by its exogamus rarity

you are troubled by many things – but only one is needed

    running 50 miles a day
        over salt roads that wd
            have tested the Model T,
              burning
                6000 calories a day &
              another 2000 on bodily
            functions on peanut butter
        & liquid curds for 2 wks
        & abscessed teeth.
        But somehow the body compensates
        & then out of the matt dusk, a storm,
        a streaming gauze in the remnant light

            the apples are round w. death in heaven
              the measure of all beauty rippling w. flesh
                & camouflage
                    the parakeet & the carpet in a demigods eye

                    The frost wd be out w. the night, & under partial
                moon in the rings of oil the novel landscape

>   moved again;
>   the stalking scrub & poplar
>   keep yr eyes on those telephone wires,
>   as the gardens behind the street follow,
>   the nexus of walls & streets & foliage shadow
>   crumple & fold. But he that is past is past. &
>   the movement continues
>   The clouds are not important,
>   any combination to the simple point
>   escape into a world where reticence & twilight
> tones aren't everythg
> did the Neanderthal lack
>   the neurons to hold the world in his head
>   drawing up his hamper of eidectic realism
>   in order to be thrust a 40 ft
>   figurehd in the spume
>   & hail, to see more

>   a performance by
>   the poetseer monkey
>   addicted to the autochthonic
> perennials tree sky water animal;
> wch is why we are irascible atavistic
> Dendrites – I cant see a fucking thing.

These are the keywds: eidectic, rimes riches, polo, dirty, candy, so-so, another. Watch out for them.

Did I tell you the flat hasnt got a stick of furniture apart fr a four-poster mattress. Nightmare is propped against the wall exactly the same spot as G when he come. *Im speeding my face off, Ray. Have y/ heard of Gurdjieff.* Her Brummie as thick as Gurdjieffs. I only know him thru Orage. Gurdjieff is the man.

Im asking her if shell be in my film & she goos all nosey Whats it about, & what does she do. I says Do y/ have aesthetic or ethical objections, & she says Whats the difference. I still dont have an answer.

But I dont understand her Foucaldian exampl of S. American trybes stimulating thir babiz genitals to sleep.

all the broken children whove been set rolling
to the boarding jetty of some vessel; the queues of shabby men bng looked over by Scotland Yd as they go down the stairs to the hull: they are interested in the hats bg worn: I have this hat. Like Hitchcocks ferry jetty. All the doubtful migrants want to hide. When it is my turn, Im dropping my peak cap, distracting the officer w. the bigger hat.

There is a cabaret a silkthighed chanteuse kissing old men. It is like she carries a secret message or role. When she escapes into the bright steps & fountained square w. crowds of vagrants & people waiting for her exit, they all applaud & cheer; & from a window in the opera house a mechanical bird trilled, & the walkie talkie keeps track

I was w/ Steve Spy agenst th same wall. & I red him som 'pms' – whoz lines may not be menciond, dey got evisserated & put into som rutines – but anyway I red him th typscript of Party Pm – & he cd get into that.

To be all th broken flotsam. Heere w/ yr nerve; owt owt ut in th pissy sae. Sooo faaar.
I sd I cd feel this nutral baeth of inocuousnes al th tym – I want to
be *mad* a free radical melting th fascia binding my heod, my class, my commonweale th cicen wyre net of a papiermasche doll

& Steve just jumpt on me – Ðeres nothing good abote bg mad!
Becuz all he cd feel when he was going into his episode was this Peine – a ship of picche dat draggd him under

so Im saying I felt trapt in the bkgrund radiaciun of langwige kultur
psyche hware a self is anihilated in histori

And hee sd, *Yeah but yre not just that!*

& w/ that kiss th bald Princ
  had set þis Princess free
      had he gnown it,
         & for da next 10 yers
           I manfully lowered my
            Rapunzel haire & set off to
          seek a laptop & a Top Shop suut
        & cam bk evry nicht to shin bak up
      my own matted haire

        & wone day y/ fand that th walls
       of yr intersecsional refuge
      werent thær & I was
        so scared I ran awey
           to London to th neerest prizon
             & askd th gaoler to lock me up agen

    hrap me up in yr cloke of intertextual fuckadoodle

dere ar a milion þings to run from – thaer ar a hunderd þings today,
a hunderd þings tomorow, thære ar a thuzand tomorows promising
disappoyment bicuze God didnt vote for yr Party –
thær ar ten billion peeple hwa dident vote for yoo –

& at th last Im running,
   at th last Im staying –
      yes & no, mann & cild,
         cwick & dedd – & at th last

        has led me to a boc ut of tyme,
          þat leves indelicasis lic Natur & Sawol
    to th birds
  a poeticks scweezed owt of the alimentarie canal
    of educasion
        O cild – yre too much of a cocanut to get a prize –
            & if y/ cd haf yr tym agen, y/ cd run a million mils
                                      fr theze
                              run fr them,
                        th ethnopoetics,
                  the liminal bollocs,
              ptics maskerading
          as bolocks bolocks
        let this run fr them,
     run fr yoo run ontill
    yr bolloks ar blew
  run frum all
hwoll publish yu

Litel doxys litel doxys
littel doxys made of tickytacky
litel doxys litle doxys
litle boxes al th same

thaer ar pink wones & yelow wons
& they al go to th seminar
to th lærners of th doxa
& dey al þink just th same

DOLDRUMS 2019/2020

all eyow Sabine wimen
stuck in pancake makup
yoo raindeered ruminants
herded into tenures
chewd down to yr denturs
lowing for revolucion
bifor yr department gets culld

dead poltroon behind yr share
Tutankhamun in a barber chaere
scared that something else will fly by
scared that something else will fly by

The prezent
    as clowd of possibilitiz
        folows y. everyware
            if you cant liv in th prezent,
                then find another prezent
                    a broncial condicioun w.
                  razberry cordial –
              gul gul gul
                th prezent as a memori of sumething ded

    a chance to fal down th stærs of th barge agen
  or fayling that bang yr heod aganst a wall again
& agaen & agan –
  if yre not banging yr hed aganst a wal
    yre not remembering riht –

               th prezent is a cloud
                  a pink nippled sucubus
                     or water tortur of want

                  th prezent a scrap of newspaper
               þat gets slapt on yr
                  papiermache carapase
               till riggid w/ wyrds
            th self as booc that sumwane els wrat
   & y/ rede yr favorit passig over
         & over agan untill th ink has
               transferrd to yr eyballs

            hwa is it reding me.

I looked for y/ in the Body Shop
I looked for y/ in the Body Shop
& God helps my mascara run

I looked for y/ in the attic
I looked for y/ in static
& 2 little Pakistani children
gobbling cauliflower on the stoop

dere ar a thuzand prezent tenets dat th prezent is al we have –
the obnoxius deere snaffles a snowdrop
a catt affixes a teliscope to its ey
a singel pointed phagosyte
Now
is God
doing stuff w/ things,
& hwen th doing is donn, yu ar fuking dedd

              hwo sez
         Im not writing 35 yrs ago,
           from an awtobahn foxhole w.
                    th Russian tanks
                      roling down to Ulm,
                 hwoo sez hes not trying
                 to hicch a ride w. th Russian tanks –
         Im writing into th futur
              ware onli cockroches ar left
                 to riffle in librariz,
              a prezent
                      dats dredging up th prezent

                I am writing into deeth,
              running to displasements
           Lands End, Soissons, Hessan,
      Bodensæ
    magicking litel girls into th lack,
       hwen al th tym I was running fr Yoo,
         as other peple wryte into th
              atheists Paradyce of beeing richte
                 th tragedie is, that sumbody must be God
                    a petulant godling hwa dozent gno
                    his task is riting th futur God
                    of blackcurrent sherbet

let me heare Yu, Allaaaah
WONE TOO THREE FORrr

I luve y/ riting luve, shyning
              thru th sugarspun of societie
         th crazed wimmen & th crazed
      men & th murderus cildren

glewd in a gravitie of luv
railing aganst ðoz hwo
poke a stick in thire
eyen & rail aganst Hu
dripping immanens sirup
tho3h written ut of histori

wat is it y/ lufe abot a pm lic Gods green appel,
lufe th wiman-gyrl & th boi-man stuck
in a scracching memori groove,
lufe th paper ðeyre printed on,
luf an idiot sweeping th peces
of his exes into a dustpan,
lof th idiot & th pan
stick sume raizins on a
toffee appel & call it by yr lof
call th toffee æppel God & love *that*,
tell Him y/ want to eate his razins
lufe yr kidney stane & if it ever cumes ut
put a ring on it
luf anything, as long as its helpless,
as long as its not a booc,
lof yr lofe even if it doznt
lofe y/ bk lufe it as an albino
a dissociatif fuge into a teenage
26 yr old who must never leve
Shangri La – but finaly left Shangri La
to turn into a sexagenarian teenager
in his prime
a slav gyrl
cawht by her do3hter & suns
can never find her way bk from th place she was born
& Hell is half her Deen

Ooooww I dont now wy the gaoler of a won hors town
has lockt herself up – wont eow cume lock me up
Wooaah I dont kno why I dont kno why
a sailer stowd away in a garden shed dat
ran agrund his hed
eou ran agrond a bed,
spinning timiditis
wont y/ cume lock me up
& in yr babiz arms y/ need no telefone
to heare yr faders ded
Ooohhh can y/ hear me now, moning to deed frends
Ooooh Im moning in bottels that wash up over
Walthamstow

Yoo ar not my owner, Yoo are nat my slav, & if it were an indeterminat
sentense, if y/ were a letter never writ, & dis a chain gang song dat
lifted clear from th rioting
a sacrifys of yr fake fur cutout hart on the Diwali bonfyre floting lost
in coeli particulats of a thusand illicit wood burners
it wil never get there
hwat is *ther*,
& hwat is *it*,
& wat is *never*
O Kaiserling herzling

Ive been chasing y/ for 13 yrs,
chasing y/ w/ wifely tears,
harryd y/ & marryd y/
fochte & nearly caw3t y/
& if y/ cd see wats its dune to Me, to loze th mann I gnew
cud burie his hatchet in Allahs heort

                              ye dont want a boc
                          of obvius delusory presense?
                      Wel Hoos asking yoo ya literal
                  gobshite –
            tie yr cateckesis to the retiform
       of a billiun spyder mynds
     fuck off & fynd
  a cultural producsion
 mor suuted to yr stacioun

Saqi,
lock th door to th selfpozessd,
cume to th lock-in lyk a cild w. fever
to th choclat licquurs & spoonfuls of elemental iron
Cume now, if y/ ete yr dinner I wil smell of Mustafa for th rest of yr lyf

I luv yr riting poynting owtside poynting upsid pointing evryware but a currensy inflated to one thuzand percent
God I luve you baby,
O BAAABY
BAAYBEE BAYBEE
th cockroches of that Day wil rite y/ out of th living
so pore yr heort ut damn th wirds
poure yr hart to deaþ

dont let ignorans stop y/ making a masterpece
Say say **say**
until it formulates a period, a peroracion, a tired old saw
a shap lic a thing on yr mantelpece
even yr mantelpece
even a walk to tak a photo
& sell it to a Foole hoo saw y/ cuming

I saw y/ coming
Say say say
free from th condicional polise
free of skill or shame
saying until y/ say it
Cume for me, Dost, Im being held in th prezent
assayled by squals of folly

I dont know how to reche y/ diamond herted mine
I dont kno how to spk to y/ w/ut mooving my lips
on this rocc I bilt a fluttering lucky bag of lickrice allsorts & gall
I dont gnow hoo you ar, hawled into th prezent a shiny fish cownter in
a supermarket gently gooing tepid under dayliht halogens
& I cant get bk to yoo
yve been wearing a dethmask for decads & its starting to slip
I dont gnow how to fix it

a thuzand words moning as I slam th door
a thowsand swerwords flaming ever more
a thuzand steps to th shops dat never leve
hwere is hame to th mann hwo always leves
hwar is luve for th wyf hwo cannot læve

shes trying to reche you w. every claw mark menses birthday card
can y/ heare her offstage whisper!
trying to reech yu till y/ heare her in Me –
feel compasion for all th qwanta of an idiot cosmos
feel compassion for th supermkt trolly & da shopper
feel compassioun for every life form strugling aganst Perfecion
wat about yoo –

I wend to th market but noboddy wd buȝ min saoul
I wend to th market but noboddy byȝd my soale
Im coming hame w/ shopping I never even stole

dont þink of the ende thenk of th step
dont thenc of th steppe thenk of th goal
dont thenc of yr foot þenc of th rode
dont þinc of th rood thinc of th frigge
dont thenc of th paine thinc of th kettel
þenc of th plage th ague th foot th Dettol
thinc of th triplefilterd milk

wil anywon giv a lift in lockdown
my rhumy olde een hav seen non sins I stopt
let me draw min bow ane last tyme
waer ere tha arrow falleþ so bury my fake fur hart
Tak me to Brent Cross on my litter
gide my skelaton hand to a pece of cardbord & stand me up on th sliprode
tape a brocen twig to my fuking thumm & let my signe sey,
He wants to see his moðer

TO THE HITCHHIKING DEAD 20??

           & at th fyrst blast of ðat daeg
        schule banes be summoned &
      ligaments & haire & a chepe
     ticcet to Snow Hill, &
   da thraed of a dozen
trowzers unwind
th rade

   & at th second blast
     th gracil foot
       beginnes its flihte &
         winds bac 20000 mils
           of venous string

              & th rades start to ravel
            th lodestar to travel

             for sheer stock drama
                 there is nothing to surpass
                the annual migration of bats
             unless its imagining her burnt
          in a ward so you forgive each other
       Hey Tigress, Ile be passive
    making use of all things anthropomorphic
     as a gangbang of seagulls around a female
       & finches harrying themselves for unguarded
      eggs

           Ic cume thru3 Wealds to th Frensshe see,
             & wayted for th next Ice aage, that micht

min birdlic banes be sent hem to Bengal,
or Basra, or Hijaz,
or hwereverY cume fro,
& all acros da Conte of Flanders
ðe invaders wer massd, Jutes & Francks,
Neanderthals & weedy homo sapiens wif
deorskin boots

Wot ar they loocing at –
do ðey want yor flat?

stand on this schor & loc at th crincled
sae of her belly, dat swelled yr cildren,
held My cildren, folded ower tales
a belly dat even holds th dedd
I can see Shangri La in yr
crincled belly

þose dark bodiz
leving th Levant
leving th Maghrib
& milling at Calais
w/ better shoos than me –
Im wayting for th sae to freez
or wayting þa catastrofhe of meltwater
let me kiss yr crincled bellig – its given eall it can
heere is a brocen bellig of a wiman – step acros her to
yr luft
heere is th brocen belig of words th brocen belly of pleding
th brocen pitted creeses of ice that refuze to melt, dat leachd
the ayre of Mercy & made a strait to drown in

dere is a bryge bitween us ymad of glacial ayre
dis endlesse deceetfull sycle of horefrost
& luve

Hwat ar yous dooing – has
anywon moovd?

stand heere
w/ ure raddled jenes
& *coyna beti* bangles, deyre al
standing on th sliproads, holding armfuls
of entrailes & a dirty pece a cardbord w/
nuffing hriten on it, & eys screwd to th horizon

hear th traffic smash by & th hwip of lorry tailwind,
& da rode blanc w/ th gasts of lorriz & cars – hwer
is th gast of petrol fums
evryone stands on thir raod, th rads to NY
Sylhet Rotterdam Darmstatt
stand ther holding entrailes
stand ðer holding
Hell

Yore standing on a rad
ðats traveling at
300000 kps
to end up at yr fate
w/ th sam suntannd bodi,
all th yunge bodiz in this body
in that bed crying It dosnt mak any
diferense!

    I haf stopt dooing,
     & th rade is dune
   theze billions
  flickering on th rode,
 frozen in a lost memori,
  hoo forgot thire last memorie –
   al dedd, al alife – hwat is ure last memori
    of bg on-life?
      þey start drifting away to thire forgoten lifs,
       þey freez on Haqq's hard sholder
        & the infinit knot of thir wyrld line
         becumeth straitend on dis rode,
         ðis rode dats alwys Shanghaid
       to th prezent
      an rade þat finaly
     reched infinitie

   an hwat do y/ remember –
  one epiphanal half minute
 on a coach ride,
of moonball mushrooms;
just one mutant stretch of them in legend
Son, watch over them, as I watch over you children
  looking for a clean floor in Edinburgh w. 3 quid to spend,
   in the only lit window outside the Royal Academy a basement
    installation a tapering chute into the middle of nothing;
     a perfect sump oil reflection of the fluorescents,
      & elegant white bannister suspending itself
      giving my milk to the park kittens
     O who will believe y/ wrote
    this before the Ribena pm!

      Ey Majnun, hwot ar y/ dg,
    biting ure tether,
  in all wether
  ut in th yard —
    circeld 3 tymes
      arond ure tail
        to settel in w/ a boc,

        Ey Majnun, eow went wilde dogge
          looking for hefor on Bodmin moor,
            & after 20 yrs ye fand her in a celler
           prinkt wif heeted unguents & candls,
         & fand lufe a wiman cauht at dawn
        utside de walls by th nicht wacche,
     cloðs torn frm her an beten

    Ey Majnun, y/ stowd away
   wif da wimmin
 sold as slavs in Yemen
to th colonial gentlman
  in linen & capsizd in th
    cwiksand of cildren

      but after al is sd & dune
      & after al is sed
      & after al

     Ðats nat yoo blustering
       in a wimans bodi, dats nat
     yoo loony in þe attic, yore nat
   th crashing saeweed of cemetarys
  caling yu to enter, yre not
God,
 yre nat even god

Yre not th husk of luve,
yre not th crumbling marrige,
 yre not th phantoms running
  ronde & rond th urn until it
   bræc –
    yre not deeth by hart dizeaz,
     yre not th morners hwo cant recall
      yre not Khandan washing th bodie
       in the masjid mortury

        lic th lichen, lik th flu,
        lyk th cosmic ray dat
        slices thru yr brain,
        yr job is to fill dis spase
       w/ Hu
      Sez th chewing gum to th shoo
     Im widYou Allah

 y/ ran & marrid th same story
  as evry other storie –
 y/ marrid Khandan,
th Saqi & th wine

Follow me, yoo lemming,
 theyr al deed, deyr al alive,
  yoo, Midnihte, Graham, Steve,
   th driver & th lorry, da hunta &
    th cwarrie
     th frends I slouff off evrie kiss,
      folow hem onto baking blyss

       a wyfman pushes out a voodoo doll
        & a Hakim sticks it w/ a pin & sets it

                    chittering on its path –
                Run, run fr them deorheart,
            run fr poizon dart,
        run w/ yr shopping cart
    run, run
    Mad G, who goos
        through his sulphate
            like a prow, getting moved on
                by the Gendarmes from summer,
                    as I am water
                        one last push in the sun

                        let him crawl to Heidelberg
                        & let hem fynd him in a cave

            in th useless sliprodes – RODES
            in th beehives – rodes & rodes
        th trees Ribenas of roze!
    cypress & planes al rodes
    all RODES
        al th wailing & AAGH
            of dis moaning is Roze
                yu ar blesst y/ profitless
                    dromedary

                I see yu fool,
                    I see y. Khandan,
                        Grayham, Midnict, Pete,
                            I see yoo Dost Dost Dost,
                            but its not you – I wawked
                            from here to th next stop –
                            but its onlie roze of
                        th roze of th rodes

                I love y/ so much
            y/ Godless punks
         I love y/ as much as
       the next sociopath
      wat use is dere
       for an Allah of th lost,
            hwat is th poynt of ðese
               peple of da boocs —
                   a clubbabel huggabel
                      Crones dizese muggabl
                         bad moðer smothering kibbutz

                     run fr ðe damnd reding Althusser
                  fr poetri an excuse for politicks
                & politicks an excuse for neuroticks
                ure nat th historie of opression
                or the fetissh of yr skin

       dere is glorie in th flyover
        & th li3ht,
           dere is glorie
              dying of plage

                     & if
               y/ hadnt coverd yr hd
          w/ yr shroud in the supermkt bay
        y/ wd haf seen My Names in th stars
       of Brittany or Hessen, & raed My playnt
       to y/,
               & if y/ hadnt buried yrself in a
                 sleeping bag in a porch in
                         Bodmin
                    y/ wd

     have seen th hidden
    trezur thru a rift in My blanket –
   & traced the ayat of My stars
   & even th acid street lamps of Bodmin
   even th Beste dat creepeth moor,
    even th porch & sleeping bag

    I trace yr fate
     & Khandans fate
     & wyfmans fate
      & a sister & a broder,
       & a clot of flesh in a clement
       fate,
        O gentle Crusher, in a flounders
        bait

       & if y/ hadnt covered yr head
      in a fascia of language, a prison
     of yr making, & yr schooling & yr
   friends
  the neverending ritual cliteredectomy
 of the tribe
y/ wd have read
the constellations on this page,
 & Allahs Hand is always writing you

    & if y/ werent all craving to get new slates
     on yr roof & a kitchen extension & a biopsy
    for the dog
     & the gd opinion of yr peers
     the right opinion for the Just
    & a sprung mattress fr Ikea

& if y/ werent all dependent
on saturation street lamps
to stop y/raping & looting in the night
y/ cd see whats good for y/ is not gd for y/
& whats bad for y/ is not bad for y/,
& what is untold suffering & predation
& the agony of soft inertia
makes a masterwork
of the World

yre running at
300000 km ps
to end up at
yr fate
w/ the same
suntanned body,
all the yng bodies
in this body, crying in bed –
It wdnt have made any difference
y/ married the same story as every
other story –
y/ married Khandan,
Radha, the Saqi & the wine
Y/ married marriage the shot-
gun the horse & the carriage
I am so looking forward
to this wedding cake,
& then I realize
its someone
I know

that body
w. a keyhole, that

                    body w. untimely breasts,
                        a birthing belly of births,
                    it all gets sucked bk down yr chute
                    w. all the charging particles & forces
                        to end up where they started – w/
                                a clot of God

                        & after all is sd & dune
                        after all is sd & don
                        all is sd & don
                        sd & dunn

                            ðe end
                        of th story is alwyz
                        th same
                      y/ alwyz haf to cume hame to luve
                     da same as evry other storie
                    exsept for thoz infermal hosts hwo syded w/
                    thire brain

                    & at th final blast an infinitessimal drop of
                                            water
                            fals to an infinit drop
                            falls fr every anngel,
                                falls to everi
                                    drop,

                                ower
                            luminessent
                        scwiggles streccht out
                        to a spoke,
                    dis man þat wyf þis cild dat lyf,

Majnun Layla prisoner & gaoler
al poynting to a perfect poynt
never to meet nor
disappoint
 & my deaþ in sleet
maks my lyf
compleet

& still
they keep faling
& stil we cannot stop

everich summer a blizzard of
midges blows owt under covir
of cottonwood schred
remake joy in dese wildes
of memorie –
ðis selfe dat self
dat now,
connecting
sent trails of th
antelope & parde,
that they meet again
in endles ambuscades
& byte eche other
in delite
Allah lyk a
carnal
luve
spoond
on a carpet
sharing sweets

www.ingramcontent.com/pod-product-compliance
Lightning Source LLC
Chambersburg PA
CBHW031347160426
43196CB00007B/767